Coolie LINES

The seafarers who could never return to India

Coolie LINES

The seafarers who could never return to India

Praveen Kumar Jha

Translated by

Pooja Priyamvada

YATRA BOOKS

An imprint of Vani Prakashan Group

vaniprakashan.com

Hardcover First Edition : 2024

YATRA BOOKS

VANI PRAKASHAN GROUP

Yatra Books is an imprint of Vani Prakashan Group

Head Office

4695, 21-A, Daryaganj, New Delhi 110 002, India
Phone : +91 11 23273167, 23275710

Registered Bookstores and Offices

Ashok Rajpath, Patna-800 004, Bihar
Coffee House Campus, Mahatma Gandhi Marg, Allahabad-211 001, Uttar Pradesh
Mahatma Gandhi International Hindi University, Wardha-442 001, Maharashtra
36A, Shakespeare Sarani, Near Rani Birla Girls College, Kolkata-700017, West Bengal

sales@vaniprakashan.in
vaniprakashan@gmail.com

Coolie Lines
by Praveen Kumar Jha
Translated from Hindi Pooja Priyamvada

ISBN : 978-93-5775-044-8
Non-Fiction

Price : ₹ 695

Printed and bound in India at IBH Print & Bind Pvt. Ltd.

Dedicated to all those seafarers
who set on an unknown voyage 200 years ago,
and could never return to their country.

COOLIE LINES

In 1826, a ship full of workers was headed towards the Reunion Island in the Indian Ocean. This was the beginning of separation of millions of Indians from their roots. Will this tale of the greed of a Herculean empire and the struggle of Indian immigrants be forgotten? How would these illiterate people survived on those islands alien to them? Will their future generations lose their Indianness?

The writer sets on investigating this migration via archives, reports in various languages and *Girmit* ancestors. He can visualise an India surrounded by conspiracy and torture, with its roots still prevalent in society. In the files from Mauritius to Canada, many such secrets lie buried, that raise questions on the British government. Also, when the same food is being cooked in a village in South America and a village in Basti, one mustn't forget that the 'Great Indian Diaspora' is a family.

CONTENT

Preface

ALTHOUGH WE use terms like 'NRI' or 'immigrant', majority of these people are 'contract workers' or doing business there. Someone may be employed at Microsoft in USA, while another may be an employee of the Medical Council of London; One may be working in a restaurant in Australia while another may be employed with some Sheikh in Dubai. If not them, it may have been their father, or grandfather or great-grandfather who migrated here. Each immigrant is in some way a *girmitiya*. Though I haven't met any actual *girmitiya* who the British masters in India had sent to different colonies, but I have met some descendants. Their history seems to have been lost or scattered. While putting them altogether, it seemed like gathering fallen leaves of a poplar tree in autumn. The more I tried to collect them, the more they seemed to scatter.

This is the history of perhaps the largest migration in the world. Thousands of hapless people were sent by ships to unknown lands by making them sign on documents which they could neither read nor understand. It is the story of the greed of one of the greatest empires in the world and the struggles of the migrant Indians. They never really got justice– people who could never return to their homeland. Their debt remains with Britain.

Besides the *girmitiya* in the Reunion Island, Mauritius, Fiji, Suriname, Caribbean Islands, East and South Africa, this book also contains the history of Malay and Myanmar. A chapter is also devoted to Sikhs, who migrated to Canada. Sources are diverse, since British historians and archives have written less about French and Dutch colonies. On the other hand, French and Dutch documents are in their language. The onus of translating them fell on modern researchers. The *girmitiyas* themselves weren't so educated to document their history. Even their next generation continued to work in the plantations. In the third generation, there were educated lot but by then the era of the *girmitiyas* was over. I contacted some of those descendants but it took time to collect the archival material and documents pertaining to them. To collate them was also a difficult task. One obvious option was to visit these islands to collect data,but it was not practical because they are scattered across the oceans of the world. The *Girmitiya* offices and depots do not exist now in India. The copies of *Girmitiya* agreements remain buried in archival files in England, France, and the Netherlands.

In many ways, this is one of the first attempts that aims at collating the entire experience of this migration. Not written by a historian but by a storyteller, it is bound to have a distinctive form. I found more questions and less answers. I shall be grateful if in the future some historian can help to find the answers. For instance, are Indians still the largest diaspora in the world? Even larger than the Jews or the Chinese or people of British origin? People of Indian origin are now spread across the world, right from Jamaica to Djibouti, uneducated villagers to nobility, Hindus, Sikhs and Muslims, From North and South India. Even after more than 200 years, this migration continues. Why are Indians found in these far-off corners of the world? What is their common history? What did India or Indians gain out of it? There is another striking question which the book tries to ask. How did casteism end for these migrants from feudal India when it could not be erased even after two hundred years? From where did these *Girmitiyas* get this strength?

Many stories in this book are incomplete. Either I could find only a part of the story or some fragmented bits. It was attempting to join them like torn pieces of paper, but I couldn't complete them. I thought even if the truth is incomplete, it should not be tampered. Most of them have been presented as they were written. As a writer I have used very little of my freedom or you can say in this writing experience, I became a bonded *girmitiya*. While I was writing this book replete with incomplete stories, I wasn't very hopeful about what shape it would take in the end. But on completion it was to my satisfaction. I felt as if by combining all the sources, I had discovered a talisman.

I am grateful to the National Library of Norway which provided several rare documents. I am also indebted to Archives of the British Library and government archives of the Netherlands, besides several articles and books written in this context. I am also thankful to young bhojpuri singer Chandan Tiwari for introducing me to the famous Sarnami singer of the Netherlands Raj Mohan. He made the journey of this book easier. My special thanks to Moti Marey and his son Pavan Marey from the Netherlands who provided me several documents and pictures for the book. There were several extended conversations and discussions with Surinamese historian and remarkable sociologist Prof. Chan Choenni about migration. Dhirendra Pal Singh introduced me to Surinamese Indian Roy Ram Sahay of Amsterdam, who kept providing me primary information over several kindred meetings. While writing this book, regular encouragement by Prabhat Ranjan and the discussions with Pushya Mitra must also be mentioned. Saurabh Dwivedi and Girendranath Jha were also a constant source of encouragement. My family and friends have always been appreciative. Ashok Kumar Pandey, Prakash Kumar Ray and Sadan Jha have a special place in such encouragements. After the publication of the original Hindi edition, appreciative review by Yatindra Mishra and the spontaneous and kindred discussion following it is unforgettable. For trusting my writing ability and offering enormous editorial support and facilitating this task, I am indebted to Vani Publication and Aditi Maheshwari Goyal. I hope this book would be useful for researchers on immigration and for laymen.

Prologue

JUNE 1970, Ba Island, Fiji

"Duniya se jaane wale jaane chale jaate hain kahan" *(People who leave the world go where, who knows).*

A song is playing on Fiji Radio and Ramdeen is lost in his past lying under the shade of a mango tree. Wearing *dhoti-kurta* and having turned his white turban into a pillow, Ramdeen is transported somewhere else in time and space. If time could be turned back, he would be perhaps lying in the same posture in his village in Bhojpur.

Ramdeen belongs to the *Chamar* caste. He would be soon 90 years old, but his arms are still strong. He tills the fields along with his sons right from morning. Now his eldest son has bought the first tractor of the village on a faraway island. Their family is one of the prosperous families in the village. Had it not been so, how else would there have been a radio set in the house?

Ramdeen was born in 1890 in the British Empire in Hindustan in some *chamartoli* in Bihar. This year of birth is fictional, but this is what it is mentioned in government documents. Ramdeen's grandfather had taken a loan from the landowner of their village in Bihar, which his descendents were paying off. His home was in the zigzag lanes among the many mud huts of the *chamartoli.* During rains, their hay roof could not stop the floor from getting wet. Just outside the hut was a trough from which the buffaloes grazed. There was a small charpoy with weared out and torn ropes and a crater shaped hole in the centre. One had to lie down carefully by placing one's legs on either side of the hole. There was an earthen pot which his mother would fill everyday from the well. Even if his caste brethren would sneak for a sip, his mother would rush at them with a broom.

The hearth was outside, obviously because it can't stay inside. The hut would catch fire. During rains, the rainwater would drip into the rice pot and the rice would taste delicious! *Babu* (father) would return tired from the landowner's fields and on his way from *Passi-tola* he would get drunk on the local liquor and eat one full plate of rice without anyside dishes. Again, at dawn when it was still dark,he would leave for the fields.

Statue of Baba and Mai, Suriname (Courtesy- Moti Mahre)

Ramdeen doesn't remember his father's face properly but says he had thick moustaches and arms of steel. He would wear a vest, a *muretha* (turban) and a black *tabeez* in his neck- *Shaneechra Tabeez.* Maa would cook thick rot is and vegetable at four o clock in the morning which he would eat before leaving. The buffaloes were also milked early morning. One glass of milk would be kept at home and the rest delivered to Yadav, who paid about sixteen *anna* a month for it.

When Ramdeen grew up he too joined his father slogging in the fields. His *Gouna*[1] had happened long ago followed by conjugal life.

1 Ceremony associated with the consummation of marriage. It is associated with the custom of child marriage.

One day, he had gone to a fair in Buxar along with Lakhanma from the neighbouring village. What could he buy at the fair? He didn't even have a penny. They sat forlornly under the shade of a tree preparing *khaini* (tobacco) when a vagabond Baba came along.

He pulled Ramdeen's hand with force and announced, "Dear Child! Calcutta is written in your fate. Go board a ship from there and all your worries will come to an end."

"I have heard a lot about Calcutta, but how can I go there, Baba?" Ramdeen asked.

The sadhu baba said, "Don' worry. I will arrange all that. Meet me on this very spot on the next full moon night. Bring your wife along."

Ramdeen felt exhilarated as if he had met with a windfall. By earning all the money from Calcutta, he could pay off all the debt of the landowner. They would own fields, do their own farming, and not remain a slave in other's farms. Ramdeen got lost in these wishful dreams.

Night before full moon, he ran away from home, along with his wife. That day in Buxar, he noticed that there were a few well-dressed government officials accompanying Baba. They were speaking in city language. Ramdeen didn't ask about salary, nor the kind of work they were supposed to do, and simply set off with the baba and the officials. City people cannot be frauds, he thought to himself. It was purely due to Baba's blessing that he had got this fantastic opportunity. They were made to stay at Buxar depot. There they met many people who later became their *Jahaji bhai* (seafarer brothers).

Ramdeen never returned home after that full moon. He didn't know that even Calcutta would be left behind and a ship would bring him to Fiji. He never heard from his father nor from Lakhanma.

But now in Fiji, Ramdeen owns a farm where he grows crops. He doesn't have to work for anyone. But he lost a lot while gaining it. Many secrets and pain lie buried in this soil of Fiji. This prosperous Island is made up of many such Ramdeens whose cries got buried with time, whose wounds dried up. Bidesiya songs are no longer heard. Letters across the seven seas are not written anymore.

Today, while listening to this song, *"Duniya se jaane wale jaane chale jaate hain kahan"* on the radio, this is what Ramdeen hazily recollects.

Den Hague, Netherlands, July 2018

"Aawa, aawa, kab aile yahan?" (Come, come, when did you arrive?)

When I met Moti Marhe first at his home, it seemed as though he had known me for years and I had played in his lap as a child. Moti's grandfather came from a village in Meerut to Calcutta and reached Suriname in 1909. This was more than a century ago but somewhere in Moti's heart, India still resides.

"Tani appan des ke meethi bhasa suni, Bhojpuri batiyabe." (Let me listen to the sweet tongue of my country, let's talk in Bhojpuri), says Moti jee.

During our conversation, he tells in Sarnami[2] that he had studied in a Hindi medium school and later became a Dutch teacher and headmaster. Years later, when he returned to Meerut, he reunited with his long-lost family. His eyes moisten as he speaks of the joy of reuniting with his land and people after two generations. His paternal grandfather was from Meerut, but his maternal grandfather was a Sikh and had come from Gujranwala (now in Pakistan).

For some time, he strolls with me in his frontyard, and it seems as if an Indian village is ensconsed in this city of Netherlands. It is strewn with leaves of colocasia and *pureni*, cucumber climbers, clay pots and a Devi statue. Speaking about these plants so authoritatively in Bhojpuri (Sarnami), he appeared to be a skilful farmer.

But deep inside this simple amiable old man, is a hidden revolutionary. Moti Marhe has been one of the inspiring figures behind the Sarnami movement, the first and only language-based movement in the history of immigration, when a collective demand

2 Moti Marhe loves to call Suriname, Sarnaam.

Author with Moti Marhe at his residence in Hague, Netherlands

for an official Sarnami language was made across two continents (Suriname and the Netherlands). Moti Marhe connected the dots between India, Suriname, and the Netherlands with one language and created Sarnami grammar.

Not just this, when Indian contribution was being erased from Surinamese history, he marked the voices of rebellion like that of Jhumpa Rajguru in the annals of history. He smiles saying that Sarnamis were teased by names like *babu* and *mai*, but he turned these words into the identity of Sarnami people. Statues of babu and mai were not only installed in Parimaribo but also in Calcutta. He digs out a few pieces of paper from his pocket to tell me how this thought occurred to him. The very words that were used to insult them, were made words of pride by him.

"You know what the other meaning of Girmitiya is? *Girna* (to fall) and *mitna* (to perish)", saying this Motiji gets emotional again.

While we were talking, his son Pavan also joined us. Pavan is a documentary filmmaker, and he has made a Dutch film titled *'Bhulal Parampara'* in which he goes to Suriname and shows the traditions of making mud pots, plastering the walls with cowdung and mud, beating wheat in a mortar and musical instruments like the *Dhol* and the *Nagada.* When one watches women in Suriname doing these chores and singing *Sohar songs* it seems as if Suriname is a small village in India. An India beyond India.

Indentured labour, Seafarers and Sailors

"Migration is a two-way process. On one hand it is the process of social and economic change and on the other a catalyst for an oncoming change for where the people are migrating to and from where they are migrating."

– C.J. Lewis•

Why do humans migrate? Why do people move to metros like Calcutta, Delhi or to foreign shores? There could be numerous reasons. But the principal reason is that there are better opportunities. Or there is some prosecution that one experiences in their place of origin. There is also a minuscule percentage of those who want to do something different, wish to experience something new. It is a global economy now but what could have happened two hundred years ago that led millions of Indians to sail across the seas and never return? How easy would it have been to leave one's village and become a *Jahaji* (seafarer)?

Who were these Girmitiya?

When I investigated the word *girmitiya*, I could not find any specific definition. According to Carter's definition, these were the contract labourers who did not have to pay for their ship journey for a specific kind of labour to a specific place[1]. This however is a simple definition. By this definition all IT employees, doctors and professionals who work abroad are *girmitiyas*. But when this term came into existence, it would have been rare that someone went abroad for

• C.J. Lewis, Human migration : A geographical perspective. (Croom Helm, London and Canberra, 1982)

job on paid expenses. These people were uneducated proletariats whose utility was determined,and work was delegated to them.

Coming back to the question, what is the origin of the word *girmitiya*?

The term 'agreement' got distorted to become *girmit* and then *girmitiya*. This agreement was made between the labourers and the recruiting agencies in British India. The word 'agreement' makes it clear that there was no coercion involved and both parties had consented. Therefore, technically it cannot be called 'slavery'. Though what needs to be observed is how capable the signatory was? Did they understand the terms of the agreement? The people who could not even pronounce this word how could they fathom what 'agreement' meant? They kept calling it *girmit* and those who signed them came to be known as *girmitiyas*. The *girmitiyas* or contract labourers were also called *kantraki* (from contract).

Why did the British designed such an agreement sending labourers to faraway islands? Why would anyone make such an expensive deal? What was the modus *operandi*? What would the government or the labourers get out of it? If there was no benefit, why would they go? Sending millions of people away could have caused massive disturbance in India. Why did the Britisher take such a huge risk? How was this whole process carried out so easily?

Let us explore its background first.

New Slavery

The history of *Girmitiya* has been written by many but Hugh Tinker has called it the 'new system of slavery'. New system of slavery?[2] Probably, even in present world, the system of slavery has changed but not the tradition.

Slaves or bonded people were essentially those people who were sold and bought, mostly without their will or consent. Till the 18th century, slavery was prevalent in the World Empires, where slaves were brought forcibly from Africa and were sold in various colonies. They had no rights and their masters made them do whatever they wanted. It was an inhuman practice which found resistance across the world (especially in London) who came to be known as anti-slavery abolitionists.

Slave trade was prohibited in Britain in 1807[3] . If slaves were found on a ship, a fine equivalent to 100 pounds per slave was imposed. But why was slavery banned? Was it because it was an inhuman practice? Why did this moral responsibility befall on the British Empire?

With the rise of capitalism in Europe, there was proportionate increase in slave trade. Slaves would often be brought from British colonies like commodities and were sold and exploited by other colonists. A nation that took pride in its moral superiority now was 'burdened' by the sin of slavery, although this thought seems a bit far-fetched. If slavery had been just confined to Britain alone it would have lasted longer or perhaps never ended!

On 1 August 1834 all slaves of the British Empire were freed, and the capitalists faced a potential economic collapse. Approximately 0.8 million slaves were set free. But what did the slaves get out of this freedom? In his Oxford Union address, Shashi Tharoor seeked an answer or compensation from the British Empire. Many like George Orwell had accused the British Empire (and his own ancestors) of covering up their mistakes. These free slaves did not get even a dime as opposed to the British capitalists who received 20 million pounds as relief! Such a huge relief amount had not been distributed for many decades in British history.•

Moreover, the slaves were made to work for five more years as apprentices, so that the work of the capitalists went on unhindered. After freeing its slaves, Britain started pressurising other colonists for the abolition of slavery. France followed suit after ten years, and the Dutch were the last to do so. Since the colonies were spread across all continents, this decision was obviously going to affect the world economy. Would this act bring capitalism on its knees? Or would there be a quest for solution? Where would 'new' slaves come from, and what would be its form? Would the solution emerge from the splendid feather in British crown-India?[4]

• In 2009 banks were granted reelief from bankruptcy

The 'new slavery' was conceptualised by one Scottish businessman William Gladstone. He thought of 'legalising' slavery. A populous country like India, burdened under feudalism for centuries, and occupied by britishers was an obvious choice.[5] Some of the issues India had, are still prevalent 200 years later.

Indian farmers were in deep distress after the Permanent Settlement Act of Bengal. Land taxes were increased, and so did the power of *zamindar* (feudal landlord). In the following decade, *Ryotwari* system was introduced in the South India which was similar to the *zamindari* system. Moneylenders became more powerful and often kept land as mortgage for loans. Farmers began to lose lands, resorting to bonded labour in their own farms. Such bonded labourers were called *kamiya.* They had three kinds of agreements. In the first agreement, they and their descendents had to work for the *zamindar* in lieu of the loan. Second type of *Kamiya* had to work through their lives but their descendents were free. Third kind had to work till their loan was repaid. However, the interest of these loans would keep getting compounded and they would never be able to repay it.

When railways were introduced in India, British goods reached even the villages and the handloom industry struggled to survive. Many small cottage industries were on verge of extinction. The foreign cloths from England were modern and much cheaper. When Oudh and Rohillakhand Railways was started, the Moradabad palanquin-bearers became unemployed. These unemployed and exploited villagers were forced to flee to the cities.[6] The place where people used to go for work was known as *Baasa* and their native places were known as *Baati.*

Lord William Bentinck remarked, "The bones of the cotton weavers are bleaching the plains of India".[7]

In Punjab, many soldiers lost job after the Afghan war in 19th century. Many of them stood on these highways, to be picked up for job anywhere in world. Unemployment was mounting while the Indian population was growing fast. The population of Madras Presidency had tripled in a hundred years. Besides, 20 per cent population in Madras comprised untouchables, who were often being sold as slaves. Bengal and southern India had been completely devastated by the hunger famines of the 19th century. Many had no other option but to migrate. People were dying in such large numbers that Lord Cornwallis had remarked[8], "One-third of our company's Hindustan has become jungle and literally a refuge for wild beasts."

The tribal people from Chhota Nagpur and Santhal hills were already working in the fields of the Bengal. They were from Dhangar, *Kol, Santhal, Munda, Uranv, Khadiya* tribes, and altogether called *Hill Coolie*. They were picked up for Assam tea plantations to cut the forests and make steps in mountains. They were made to do hard work for a paltry a sum of three rupees monthly, in which they had to manage residence, food and healthcare.

About tribal people, Ms Gillanders Company wrote on 6 June 1836 to William Gladstone,

"In the last two years we have sent about 2000 Indians on a contract of five years to Mauritius. We don't think that sending to West Indies could be a problem. It is easy to entice them. Consider the *Dhangar* tribals as apes not humans. They have no religion, no education, and no state. They just need to eat, stay and sleep and for this they can go anywhere."

Unfortunately, many of these issues are still prevalent. Existential dangers are looming before the small-scale industries, condition of farmers is pitiable, and unemployment is evident everywhere. The migration from *Baati* to *Baasa* continues.

In 1900, India's population stood at about 300 million. Among them, 30 million people had migrated out of India from 1834 to 1937.[9-10] About ten per cent of the people! It would give a rough conjecture of about 100 million Indian descendents in these countries. However, amongst these 30 million people, only about 1 million went to far off countries. The rest migrated to neighbouring countries like Malay, Myanmar, and Sri Lanka,[11] of whom many returned back.

To understand this process, we have to travel back in time to Calcutta, the commercial hub of British India. Calcutta had several recruitment agencies at that time. When demand rose for *Girmitiya* workers they hit a jackpot. Among these agencies one of the first to be contacted by William Gladstone was another Scottish owned Ms.

Gillanders Arbuthnot Company.• Gillanders Arbuthnot Company made an agreement between British agents and labourers. British Government did not expect that this process of recruitment could be done so easily in such an organised manner. Many such companies emerged later, for instance, the Gladstone Willy Company.[12]

India was in some way or the other a mine of talent even then. At that time workers would go in loincloths and now go as 'blue-collared' professionals.

Kantraki or Girmit

The Agreements were in English but were translated in either Hindi or Urdu. Although, it was quite detailed, but the workers were mostly illiterate and didn't comprehend all the terms. The agreement went like this-The indentured labourers shall go to some island to work in sugar cane fields. They would earn better wages than Hindustan: for instance, men would get 25 cents and women would get 16 cents daily. Work would be 45 hours a week but during the harvest time it could stretch up to 54 hours. Sunday would be a holiday. The agreement had four main clauses:

1. The worker and the agent shall present themselves in front of a special officer of the British Government and sign the agreement (put a thumbprint).
2. The Agreement would be for five years which can be then extended for another five years after that.
3. After the expiration of the agreement the labourer were to be sent back to Calcutta.
4. Whichever ship takes them shall have arrangements for food and hygiene and have a doctor on board.

However, the conditions varied for each *Girmitiya* island. Mauritius had an initial agreement for one year which was later changed to three

• Now, Ms Gillanders Arbhutnot company is owned by descendents of late G.D. Kothari, and known as Kothari Group Of Companies.

years. The agreement for West Indies was for ten years. Thus,recruiting them for Mauritius was easier. Although in West Indies islands like Trinidad, life was considered better, and many were sceptic about longer contracts. *Girmitiya* agent of West Indies wrote a letter from Madras that the duration there must be decreased but this never materialised.[13]

Here I would like to cite a difference between the contract labour from China and India. China was an undemocratic monarchy back then. British were struggling to get control over China, while they already ruled India. Chinese mind was still a puzzle for Britishers, but they have studied Indian minds well. The Chinese *Girmitiyas* were smarter. They negotiated the agreement in advance and each Chinese labourer would have a different contract. Chinese workers even got 'trial period' during which they could get the terms of work changed or terminate the contract. Chinese workers in West Indies had 7.5 working hours whereas Indian workers had to put in between 7-9 hours. Indians were promised a free return ticket while Chinese had to pay their return fare. Chinese women weren't bound to work while both Indian men and women had to work.[14]

Now let me introduce you to the vital link of this process – *Arkaati*.

Arkaati

"The immoral Arkati said Fiji is heaven on earth
While being under the sky it is still on the top
I ask if Fiji is Heaven, where is hell
It isn't hell but conditions are worse than hell"[15]

The local recruitment agents who brought workers were known as *Arkaati*. Initially their work was easy like that of the agents of some Ponzi schemes. They would go to the villages and lure people saying that we are taking you to heaven. But eventually the youth of the villages came to know the truth and *Arkaati* became the target of the village elders and *zamindars*.

The *zamindars* never wanted their workforce to move out of village. *Arkaati* agents had to change their *modus operandi*.

Agents would not meet potential indentured labour in the village instead, they would call them to small towns. They would meet them secretly in some countryside fair, temple, or highways. They would hunt down youth searching for jobs in cities. They would spot somebody who seemed lost or absent-mindedly standing in a corner. People who spoke a lot, laughed loudly, or posed as leaders were not picked. These gullible people were shown a utopian world. The agents would boast of having contacts with the big recruitment firms for sending abroad. These unemployed hopeful youth would beg them to make some arrangement. Some youths would even steal from homes or sell cattle to bribe these agents.[16]

But many Indians didn't want to leave their homes. They loved to eat whatever they got in their villages even though it was meagre. Breaking the family ties was difficult, especially in the areas of Bihar (Bengal State) and UP (United Province). They lived in closely knit communities. There were many levels of their attachments ranging from village deities to their cows and mango trees. Many were worried how could a suitable groom be found for their daughter, in a foreign land. What kind of dowry will he demand? What if their daughter remained unmarried for her entire life? And if they die there, who will perform last rites? How will they attain salvation unless village priest does so?

A ship journey to foreign lands was a taboo and it meant *Kala Pani* (Black waters). If they were to return,they would be considered out castes in the village. They would have to return only after the purification rituals. The decision whether they are fit to be back in the village or not was to be made by the village elders. The *Baudhayan* religious formula popular amongst Hindus back then had seven sins listed as prohibited and all these codes got violated in this journey. Brahmins had seven taboo 1. Travelling by ship 2. Getting involved in any business 3. Stealing another Brahmin's property 4. Giving wrong information about land 5. Serving someone from a lower caste 6. Making a woman from a lower caste pregnant 7. Being born from such a womb.[18]

But such taboos were not across whole India. Punjab didn't have this concept of Black waters. In three districts of Bihar Shahabad (Arah), Patna and Saran, it wasn't strictly a taboo.[19] The environment in Gaya district was also changing.

Not everbody left for money.[20] Some had conflict with the family, or they were passionate to do something new, or were orphans, abandoned or widows. In the beginning of 20th century, daily wages for labourers had also increased in India. The British rulers we reconstructing roads, laying down railway lines, setting up industries. In Bombay and Calcutta, labourers made a decent amount of money. In this scenario the reason for going abroad could not have been just money. They must have been promised other incentives.

One upper caste *Thakur* of Fiji had some differences with his sister-in-law and he left home. These issues were trivial, but *Arkaati* caught them at right moment.[21] A Brahmin youth named Devi Sharan Pathak fell in love with a girl from a lower untouchable caste. The village *panchayat* outcasted him, his beloved hanged herself from a tree and her father was lynched by the villagers. Ashamed and depressed, he left for Fiji. His name in Faizabad depot was entered as Debi Saran from a lower caste *Kumhar*.[22]

Many tricks were played to trap them.[23] If somebody appeared illiterate, they were told Fiji is a place near Calcutta where you will make plenty of money. With smarter youths, a corrupt version of agreement was mentioned. Educated people were also lured about getting office assistant, interpreter, or instructor jobs for better salary. They were asked not to tell anyone at home. Most of these labourers ran away from their homes without even saying goodbye to the closed ones.

A song of protest that was sung against *Arkaati* goes–

"O re Arkaati, you've a black heart
You tell lies
Though your language is sweet & appears truthful
All you do is destroy and defame
You ruin our good name." [24]

After the Sepoy Mutiny of 1857,many rebel soldiers were dismissed from service and the rebellion. When these soldiers came to know about this scheme, many of them voluntarily came to these agents, fearing that they would be sent to prison anyway. They reached the depots of Shahabad, Patna, Gaya or Gazipur and pleaded with agents to be sent away from the country.

Many unemployed youths flocked to near by cities that were known as *Naakas*. Kanpur, Delhi, and Lucknow were big *Naakas* from where recruitment was easier. Many pilgrims came to Allahabad, Faizabad, Mathura and Benares and would be lured by *Arkaati*. Many were picked from the Sonepur cattle fair. *Arkaati* would simply roam about asking random men, "Do you want a job?" As soon as someone showed some interest, they would trap them.[25]

Mainpuri was a stop-over for child widows on their way to *Vrindavan*. A *Sehajiya* cult was growing there, which claimed to attain God by having sexual relations. Many such widows were recruited from this area.[26] Prostitution was also thriving business in Calcutta. From 1853 to 1857 it has increased from 3% to 7%. Prostitutes here were divided into three categories. One catered to the British soldiers, another to the British officers and the third category for Indian soldiers. When the Communicable Diseases Act was promulgated, they began to flee Calcutta as their private parts were checked forcibly, infamously called 'instrumental rape'. Prostitutes were relatively independent with no families, and thus an easy catch. Despite the reluctance of the estate owners to take them, *Arkaati* recruited them to fill their target.[27]

An *Arkaati* agent would get 45 rupees for each male and 55 rupees for each female they recruited. There business was going well, but things changed when a letter about a woman named Kunti arrived from Fiji. It wrote about the landowner in Fiji forcing himself on her, when she had escaped and jumped into the river. This letter was a press release in India on 10 December 1913. (Annexure 2)

One folk song that became quite popular in those times goes as follows: -

"When the oppressors were determined to
Corrupt the dharma of the Satis

In the waters jumped Kunti
Do something about this fall
Across and not afloat
May every Kunti's life be a success
Without engraining dharma
There can be no news of peace and joy."[28]

The ambience in villages changed after the arrival of her letter. Villagers would be on guard and if any *Arkaati* was caught he would be punished. In many villages there was this rumour that *Girmitiyas* were made to hang upside down as punishment and oil was extracted from their head, which they called *mimiyai ka tail.*[29] There was also news that labourers are forced to eat beef and pork and they were forcibly converted to Christianity. *Arya Samaj* ascetic Swami Satyadev delivered speeches in Muzzafarpur and Darbhanga and asked people to be wary of these Arkaatis. One Purusuhottam Das distributed booklets to make people aware of this danger.

Yet *Arkaatis* continued their hunt in towns and cities. Police and government officials were complicit with them. Let me give an instance. One day a cobbler named Ganga pleaded to Rev. Ivans that contractor Baldev held his aunt and ten more women in Khuradabad, and they would be taken to *mirich desh* (Mauritius). When the reverend asked to free them, Baldev told him that he would complain to *bada sahib.* Baldev had a license for recruiting and knew the higher authorities. Though Baldev agreed later but this was clear that the system was being regulated and encouraged by top authorities.[30]

It is important to understand the complete hierarchy of process. The highest authority called Protectors of Immigration were based in Calcutta and Madras. Their subordinates were the immigration agents of various colonies, and the district magistrates of Indian districts. Then there were licensed and unlicensed *Arkaati* agents in the lowest rung. It did not take much effort to be a license agent. One had to pay a fee of ten rupees, seek the magistrate's permission and licence could be obtained by the 'Protector of Immigration' placed in Calcutta or Madras. License-bearers would often break the rules. Licenses of 27 agents were cancelled in 1898, out of which one was even accused of rape and murder. Some agents had brought Nepali workers which was illegal. Rest were minor cases of fraud.[31]

Arkaati agents would trap the *Girmitiya* and bring them to a sub-depot (recruitment office) where they would be help captive until licensed agents presented them to the district magistrate. This process was protected by the British law (Indian Act13, 1864). According to a magistrate of Gazipur, if anyone retracted to sign the agreement, the *Arkaati* agent would tell them, "Alright! Go wherever you want, but you must pay for our expenses. You will have to leave all your money, *lota* (water pot) and *duppatta* (stole)".[32]

When they all would concede defeat, they were taken to the magistrate. *Arkaati* tutored them to say 'yes' to every question the magistrate asked. They were handed a form in which they were required to fill their name, father's name, address, and age. Name of depot, salary and the proposed duration of the contract was mentioned on the form. They would queue up in front of the magistrate. Each would say 'yes' and without even reading or understanding the agreement, they would put a thumbprint. Sometimes the magistrate would get suspicious and deny the applications too. But such occasions were few.

Disputes started right from the subdepot. For instance, Brahmins would not want to eat with Dalits (lower castes). This is one reason why Brahmins were not preferred to be *Girmitiya* but once caught would not be allowed to get away either. Many poor Brahmins on the other hand wished this job and were ready to sacrifice their sacred thread and caste. The responsibility of hiding the caste of these people was also that of the *Arkaati*. They would keep their hands soaked in lukewarm salt water for hours to make them rough, so that they could pretend that these weren't the soft hands of a Brahmin.

Arkaati were paid better for women, so they would never let them go out of hand. Some would plead and cry at the recruitment office. But they also feared that if they returned to their villages, they would be declared outcaste. There were some women *Arkaati* to sympathise with them. Many widows or harassed married women would come voluntarily, and never complained. *Arkaati* also had women spies in the village. When women would come to the well to fetch water, they would listen to their banter and carry the information to the *Arkaati* agent.[33] Later, they would facilitate a secret meeting in a temple. It isn't that women did not work in the fields in India,but on the island their wages would come directly into their own hands. This semblance of freedom enticed many women, especially widows.

Most women recruits were from upper caste whereas among men they were from lower castes. For instance, in 1898 two-thirds of upper caste *Girmitiya* were women.[34] What could be the reason for this? Were the conditions of Brahmin and Kshatriya women worse? Especially widows? Was it a fact that after the demise of their husband their condition would worsen, and they had to do several lowly tasks? Did the life of a lower caste woman did not change much after the death of their husband?

There are many stories of widows. One woman went around begging after the demise of her soldier husband. One *Arkati* asked her that despite being from upper caste why did she succumb to begging. She told him about her hardships, and he bought some *anjeer* (fig fruit) for her son. She agreed at once to sign the agreement. In 1905 that women left for Guyana with her son. One can imagine the situation how for just a handful of figs someone would be ready to go on such a long journey. This was the epitome of poverty and helplessness.[35]

Calcutta Depot and renouncing Caste

During recruitment, no experience or skill was considered. Whether someone was a *Chamar* (cobbler), *Ahir* (cowherd/sheepherd), gardener, tailor or even a priest, all would get recruited irrespective of whether they have worked in a field or not. They were not born coolies but were transformed into coolies.[36]

Whereas Brahmins didn't want to eat with the Dalits, even Dalits were hesitant to eat alongside Brahmins. They had been taught from birth to respect upper caste people. They thought that eating with Brahmins was a sin and if the Brahmin would curse them, they would never get salvation. But with time both the groups realised that in this slavery they had to support each other. The chains of caste broke and in this collective slavery a new brotherhood emerged. All castes would sing and dance together and play *Gatka* (an ancient martial art). What couldn't be achieved in many decades in India, just happened organically in few days.

From subdepots, they would be taken by train to Calcutta where they were kept in the building at 15 Reach Road. This depot was specifically for Demerara (Guyana). Mauritius depot was in Bhawanipore. Depots of other islands were in Chitpur and Ballygunj.[37] These depots had high boundary walls, which were difficult to cross and escape. There would be officers and doctors inside the depot. The depots were so big that at one time people for two ships could be accommodated there. It would be a confused lot of people from different subdepots and states.

When I tried to find the history of this depot, I came to know some interesting facts that narrate the tale of India from its glorious golden period to the age of slavery. After his defeat at the hands of the British, the Nawab was ousted from Oudh and settled in Calcutta. He built palaces on the banks of Hooghly river, and hold his court there. After his death, British appropriated it. Shrubs and bushes had grown around the huge walls of this abandoned palace, and it became a den of poisonous snakes. The same palace was turned into a *Girmitiya* depot. At Nawab's 'Bear Park', sick *Girmitiyas* were held for quarantine. The affluence of these buildings had faded and the 'Hindustan of Nawabs' had become the 'Hindustan of *Girmitiyas*'.[38]

After being brought to Calcutta the recruits were given a bath and new uniforms. A communal bath in the river Hooghly would wash away the caste differences. *Brahmins* would shed their holy thread in the flowing water. With this thread, many would shed off their caste and religion forever. The workers were also groomed in the depot so that they could fetch a good price. When some of them were given the foreign soap to bathe, a few ate it up thinking it be a sweet dish. The extent of ignorance and poverty can be estimated from this itself that people had never seen a soap before.[39] After bathing and donning their uniform, all Girmitiya would look identical. Those going to West Indies would get warm clothes because of stormy cold winds under

Southern tip of Africa, notoriously called Pagla *Samundar* (Mad Sea). Men would get woollen pants or dhoti, red woollen cap and jacket. Women would get a saree, two cotton jackets, a woollen petticoat or *pajama.*[40]

The lyrics of a folk song from those times went thus: [41]

"When we reached Calcutta, our miseries increased
They removed our clothes, garlands, and holy thread
Made us wear Bengali rags
Made the beards of ascetics
Sadhu, Dom, Chamar or Bhangi
They forced us all in one room together"

They would also get a *lota*, a tin plate and a tumbler. In the initial days, they were given money to buy food from the market but later this tradition was discontinued. The reason being that some *Girmitiya* would never return from the market. Later a contract was made with the nearest grocery shop who would deliver the supplies to the depot.

In the depot, they would be served four *chapatis, imli chutney* and jaggery or sugar. There were also arrangements for beetle nut and tobacco. Before they boarded the ship there would be an elaborate meal, just like lambs before their slaughter.

There would be health check-ups too. First by an Indian doctor and nurse and later by an English Surgeon General, though this check-up was only a formality. Usually if anyone had no disability, they would be declared fit. People suspected of sexual diseases like syphilis would not be sent. Thankfully there was no sexual check-up or instrumental rape for women.[42] They would also be vaccinated for smallpox (*Badi Mata*) which was common in those days in India.

Seafarers Move On

When each *Girmitiya* would board the ship there would be a numberplate hanging from their neck like a prisoner. It was called a 'tin-ticket'. It would remain hanging for the entire journey. This number was their identity.

While boarding the ship there would be a myriad of emotions. Some would be sad; some would be numb and some happy. Some would look for a way to escape in the last moment. One sick woman refused to board the ship as she felt she would die on the ship, but she was forcibly made to board. She jumped off the ship and died. In 1882, 15 people jumped off from the ship *Poona1*. Initially they would drown and die but later a lifeboat of the British would sail along for some distance trying to save them.[43] On the other hand, there is a mention of a widowed woman called Muniya who was stopped in Calcutta under the suspicion of a sexual disease. Muniya stole someone else's pass and ticket and boarded the ship. When she was caught later, she said that her sister Ramdaiyya was on the ship, and it was important to accompany her. She was allowed to proceed. Muniya was possibly amongst those women who wanted to exit from India at any cost.[44]

On the Fiji ships one *bidesia* song was popular– [45]

Crying in a sailing ship,
How it would be across the Black waters O bidesia?
My heart fears. No shore in sight.
Many days and months have passed, bidesia
Now I see the shore of the Fiji Island
I feel so sad O bidesia"

Generally, each ship had two decks. The upper deck was for the officials etc. and the lower deck for the *Girmitiya*. Since the lower deck would be submerged in water, so it was poorly ventilated. Each Girmitiya would get a space of 6 x 6 x1.5 feet (in some ships 6 x 6 x 2 feet) to sleep. With time the engines of the ships became modernised, and space also improved, making the journey more comfortable.[46]

To curb the caste difference issue on the ship, upper caste people would often get the job of a storekeeper or cook. Lower castes would eat the food cooked by the upper caste as a *prasad* (food from God). In 1887 on the ship Foyl some *Kshatriyas* (warrior caste) under the leadership of Podrath Singh killed themselves by jumping off the ship because an untouchable had touched them. Many Muslims had objection about a Hindu cook preparing the meals.[x47] In 1891 on the ship Jurra heading to Jamaica, 20 Muslims threw away some lamb meat because it had been cooked by a Hindu. They wanted *Halal* meat which Hindus don't cook.[48] The famous linguist and administration officer Grierson had written about food on the ship:–[49]

"A person can eat anything on board a ship. This ship is like *Jagannath* temple where there is no difference of caste."

There was also objection to the same thermometer being put into everyone's mouth, irrespective of caste. Especially a thermometer from a Muslim's mouth was unacceptable by Brahmins. But, thermometer was pushed in their mouth. A few Brahmins continued to wear their sacred thread, wear a long mark on their forehead and a holy garland. But gradually the caste system disappeared on *Girmitiya* ships.[50] However the gender difference remained. Queues for food and sleeping arrangements were separate for men and women.

They would get tea and biscuits for breakfast, but many *Girmitiya* would not be able to eat it. Some thought that biscuits were too hard. This was the 'dog biscuit', which Britishers kept for their dogs. *Girmitiyas* would get a fixed quota of water, usually two bottles of water every day.[51] Food consisted of rice, curry, dried fish, or tinned meat. Many North Indians would not be able to eat dried or tinned meat. A potato gravy would be made for them. South Indians would usually eat everything. Later, some sheeps were also carried on the ship for fresh meat.

Some provisions were made for local preferences. Especially for people from the Bhojpuri speaking belt, puffed rice, gram and jaggery was made available. *Sattu* (gram flour) was also made available. Arrangements were also made for tobacco and lime. Pregnant women and lactating mothers were given one glass of milk every day. Later they were given porridge too along with it. People from the Bhojpuri belt would prefer *chapaati* than rice. In the evening it was popular to have roasted puffed rice. Till Calcutta depot there was also *paan* (betel leaves) available, but it wasn't possible to preserve paan on the ship.[52]

The ship had a fixed routine. One had to wake up at 6 am, breakfast was at 8 a.m. Some people would have cleaning duties in rotation, and the rest were engaged in singing, dancing, or playing. Gradually all began to forget their sorrows and get used to the ambience. They would call each other *Jahajee* (ship brothers). Women would be called *Jahajin.* This relationship would now remain for years and centuries, much stronger than the blood relations.

It was on the ship itself that the display of everyone's skills would begin. The ones who appeared like leaders would be made heads. These were people who had come after running away at their own will. They were happy and would flatter the Englishmen. Totaram Sanidhya mentions the tasks on a ship in his book. There the *Girmitiya* were asked to pick a task. Many people listed themselves for *Topas*. They did not know what it meant but assumed it must be an easy task. It was the job of manual scavenging i.e., of carrying excreta manually. Many refused, but they were forced to do it.[53]

A few strange people too boarded these ships. In 1895 one young woman boarded the ship Erna with her servant, who was allegedly the princess of Nepal, who wanted to see the world.[54] This couldn't be proven in investigations, and she was sent back by the next ship to India. In 1870 several *nautch* (dancer) girls boarded the ship to Suriname who would travel from one village to another there and perform dances.

The punishments on the ship were symbolic and weird. When two people would fight, they would be tied back-to-back using a *dhoti*. If someone abused, he would be asked to stand with his tongue out for a long time. If somebody committed theft his face would be blackened and he would have to run around like a headless cock, and others would be asked to laugh aloud at him. After a certain age such insult is difficult to bear.[55] Many would kill themselves by jumping off after such humiliation.

For instance, the kind of punishments meted out in the ship *Allanshaw*[56]

1. One black officer boxed and kicked *Kalu* and the cook.
2. *Aantu* was hit with a whip.
3. *Jogeshar* and his wife were abused a lot by Robert Ipsen.
4. John Smith hit *Palukaghan* with a whip.
5. O'Brayn threw a six-pound mutton tin on a *Girmitiya* woman.

6. Willaim Clientsworth chopped off the thumb of a *Bihari*.

Since the journey was so long, rations were bound to fall short. Many lost weight and appeared like a measly skeleton. Many would keep throwing up whatever they ate on board. The journey was stinky, and the coolies were made to live in that stink. Some couldn't bear it and died midway. When the stink of the dead body reached the *Sahibs*, they got the bodies thrown into the sea. In order to curb depression spreading on the ship on such occasions, often educated people like Brahmin Devi Sharan or Munshi Rehman Khan would read aloud from the *Gita or Ramcharitmanas*.[57-58]

Many people would lose their mental balance on this trip. Many would become very quiet while many others would always seem angry and irritable. In 1892 on board the ship *Volga*, a woman Fuljhadi began deteriorating mentally day by day and would get terribly violent. By the time they reached Guyana she was declared insane. Probably she spent the rest of her life in a mental asylum. Likewise, in 1875 a woman named Ratni went mad and in a fit of anger threw her baby into the sea.[59] When this was the effect on the ship what would it be like on a foreign land? How many would survive?

Though historians believe that ship conditions may seem harsh for privileged people of today, we must remember that these seafarers were the people of the struggling and pitiable class from the 19th century. It is quite possible that for them even if the life, food, and facilities on the ship weren't luxurious they were at least satisfactory.[60] If it wasn't pleasant, why would people keep going back?

A marriage tradition also started on the ships. The ship captain and the plantation owners wanted that people become couples on the ship itself. They would ask the men,"Who would cook for you" and the women, "Who would protect you? So, choose your partner here itself". The captain himself performed the marriage ceremony. On a ship to Trinidad many such couples were formed, and marriages solemnised. However, upon reaching the island many women refused to acknowledge their husbands. Afterall, they had run away from India to get free of these marital bonds.[61]

New country, New Soil

After alighting from the ship, they were quarantined on an island for about a month. Finally, they were bathed, and assigned a unique number plate. They were clicked half naked, as an advertisement to the plantation owners could choose the labourers, based on their height, and built. Here there would be a new registration and a formal contract was drawn. This contract could be different too from the Indian contract as per local requirements and laws. This was clearly a fraud with them, but they would not know the difference.

All of them were housed in barracks called 'Coolie Lines'. Often people belonging to different castes and religions were put together in one small room. An upper caste Brahmin may be housed with lower caste *Chamars*.[62] British wanted that all caste differences would dissolve on this island, and these circumstances did help to erase the differences.

Food arrangements on the islands were different in each place. In Mauritius, food was free. In Trinidad, it was free for two years and in British Guyana, for four months. On most islands of the West Indies, they wouldn't get free food supplies, but they would get a separate allowance for it. In Fiji they would get 10 *chhatank* flour (750 grams), two *chhatank Arhar Dal* and half *chhatank* ghee.[63] But this arrangement was only for six months.

Salary was also given in Mauritius at the end of the month, while they were paid on weekly basis in Jamaica and British Guyana[64] and fortnightly in St. Louis and Trinidad. The hours of work in Mauritius were 9 hours for weekdays and two hours on Sundays. In West Indies also work hours were 9 hours while Sunday was a holiday, but one had to work only for 280 days in a year. In British Guyana it was lenient with 7 hours of work every day, Saturdays and Sundays were holidays.

Absence from work for three consecutive days in Mauritius would lead to three months of imprisonment, while in Trinidad they received one week of imprisonment. In British Guyana five days of absence could mean two months of imprisonment.

Women tried to get a partner who had been on the island for many years and were somewhat wealthy. As per records of 1838 out of the

32 women who gave birth to children there, 27 had their husbands who were better off and living there from long.[65] Women didn't have to pay dowry, instead they received expensive gifts from the groom. Some fathers would purposely get their young daughters married to get some money.

In the subsequent years many people did return to India after finishing the contract, but there was nothing for them in the village. There was no land, no respect, and no caste for them. The society wouldn't accept them back and their families would think they have returned for their share of property. When a *Kanyakubja* Brahmin named Girdhari Lal returned to India, his brother took away all his money. The villagers organised a *panchayat* and ordered a 'purification' ceremony and a huge meal for several villages with heavy expenses. He couldn't arrange all this, so he was thrown out of the village. Later he wrote a letter to a friend in Fiji who had saved some money and called him back there in 1914.[66]

The condition of women was even worse. It was considered that these women lost their dignity by travelling abroad. A woman named Mathura was sent back due to a disability, but she pleaded and went back on the ship *Albey* in 1893.[67]

Here, I would also like to discuss the plights of tribal girmitiyas called 'Hill Coolies'

A letter dated 11 January 1839 mentions, "Hill coolies were used to marshy soil, less wages and less food. They are better than Negro labourer. They appeared to be hale and healthy in Mr. Gladstone's field. Some of them married local negroes."

They weren't hale and healthy at all. In the first nine months only 38 out of 419 died, and a girl child was murdered! On 11 October 1838, two tribals named Jammo and Paltan ran away and and later their dead bodies were found at a place called Meheka. In a letter dated 2 May 1839 there are accounts of many eyewitnesses. Alexander writes, "If these coolies try to run away, they are tied and whipped". In the same letter Elizabeth Caesar adds, "Salt is rubbed into their wounds, and they cry a lot."

A witness from Guyana's hospital wrote this description–

"There is a stinky environment here, where there are no mattresses to lie down. The coolies slept with a few rags under their head. In one room, two out of five hill coolies have died. The bones of the third protrude in such a manner that he will not survive for many days. In the name of food one brown biscuit is given. Their boils have ruptured and become stones. Their flesh has dried. Their toes have gangrene and are falling away. I have never seen such a heart wrenching scenario anywhere."

A manager named Jacobs was fined 20 sterlings and a month's imprisonment for atrocities. Later, the same manager was fined 30 sterlings and 40 sterlings for his persistent complaints. In stead Jacobs collected 28.5 dollars from poor laboureres, promising them that he will stop torturing them! When this news reached India the Governor General prohibited taking the hill coolies to West Indies.

Returning was difficult because returning ships were fewer. As ship advertisements were flashed from Suva (capital of Fiji), many Indians would throng to the ships. It would be a chaos with people pushing around. There is one incident that one passenger plucked a lemon from the house of a British man on the way to his ship and his ticket was cancelled. He couldn't return to his country because of a lemon![68]

Gradually *Girmitiya* felt a sense of belonging to this new soil. They and their descendents probably never set foot in Hindustan ever again. Often in diaspora festivals they are offered a PIO card, but do they still like to call themselves Indians? Do we Indians wish to be connected to them? In next chapters, I would attempt to reconstruct such connections. Let's see how far has wings of Hindustan spread itself. The wings we call A Great Indian Diaspora!

Timeline

1728 – Some slaves of the French left for Mauritius from Pondicherry.

1798 – Permanent Settlement Act was passed in Bengal and *Zamindars* and *Rajas* were given the responsibility to collect taxes.

1807 – A Sale and trade of slaves was legally banned in the British Empire.

1812 – *Ryotwari* tradition was introduced in South India which can be said to be the equivalent of the Permanent Settlement Act of Bengal.

1815 – Farquhar, the first Governor of Mauritius brought some prisoners to Mauritius.

1826 – France took labourers to Reunion Island from Pondicherry.

1833 – (23 August) A The act for the end of the tradition of slavery was passed in the British Parliament.

1834 – (1 August) A British slaves were released, but they were allowed to be retained as apprentices for a few years.

1834 – (2 November) - *Bihari* labourers were bought to Mauritius aboard the ship *Atlas*. This day is celebrated as Diaspora Day in Mauritius.

1838 – Even apprentice slaves were freed in the British Empire. The first ship *Whitby* sailed for British Guyana.

1845 – The first ship for Jamaica named *Maidstone* and first ship for Trinidad *Fatel Razakk* sailed.

1848 – Slavery was ended in the French Empire

1849 – The duration of a *Girmitiya* contract was made three years in Mauritius by an ordinance. Earlier it was for one year only.

1853 – India had the first train and that brought a specific kind of unemployment to smaller towns. Trains also became a mode of migration.

1857 – Many soldiers were rendered unemployed after the Sepoy Mutiny.

1863 – Slavery tradition ended in the colonies of the Dutch.

1873 – Ship *Lalarukh* reached the Dutch colony Suriname.

1879 – Ship Leonidas reached Fiji from Calcutta.

1884 – Ship Syria that had sailed for Fiji from Calcutta sinks.

1905 – Ship *Eritrea* that had sailed from Madras reached Seychelles.

1910 – Sending *Girmitiyas* to Mauritius was stopped.

1913 – The letter of Kunti the *Girmitiya* from Fiji was released to the press in India. Surendranath Banerjee raised the matter of the deaths in Guyana's Rosehall rebellion.

1916 – Badri Maharaj, the first Indian *Girmitiya*, became the member of Fiji Legislative Council.

1920 – Indians in Reunion Island begin to get French citizenship. Fiji and other islands began to free the *Girmitiyas*.

1972 – Edi Amin ordered the expulsion of 80 thousand Indians.

1999 – Mahendra Pal Chaudhary became the first Indian origin Prime Minister of Fiji.

B– Belize
F– Fiji

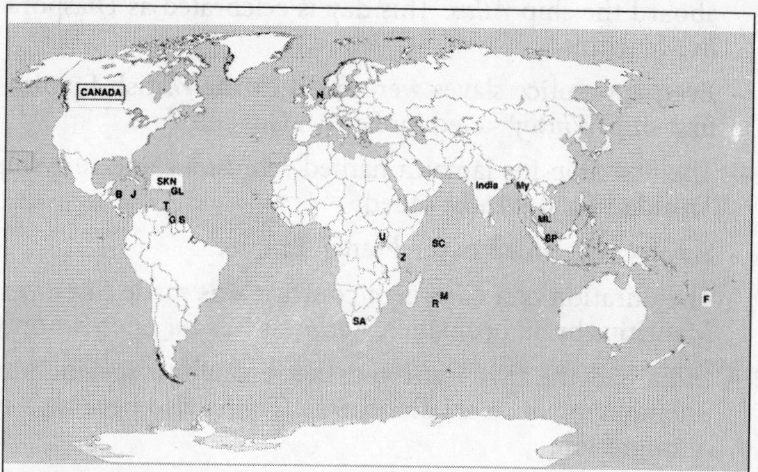

G– Guyana
GL– Guadeloupe
J– Jamaica
M– Mauritius
My– Myanmar
ML– Malaysia
N– Netherlands
R– Reunion island
S– Suriname

SA– South Africa
SC– Seychelles
SKN– Saint Kitts and Nevis
SP– Singapore
U– Uganda
Z– Zanzibar

References

1. Marina Carter, *Voices from Indenture,* Experiences of Indian Migrants in the British Empire, Leicester University Press, 1966
2. Hughes Tinker, *New System of Slavery, The Expert of Indian Labour Overseas, 1830-1920,* Oxford University Press, London, 1974.
3. Gillean KL, *Fiji Indian Migrants,* Oxford University Press, Melbourne,1962
4. Tinker, New System of Slavery, op cit.
5. Walton Luk Lai, *Indian Labour Caribbean Sugar: Chinese and Indian Migrants to the British West Indies 1838-1918,* The Johns Hopkins University Press, Baltimore, London, 1993
6. Carter, Voices from Indenture, op. cit.
7. Walton Lai, *Indian Labour Caribbean Sugar,* op. cit., Reference v
8. C. Kondapi, *Indians Overseas 1838-1949,* Indian Council of World Affairs,1951
9. Rajjinder Bhagwanbali. Contracten voor Suriname: Arbeidsmigratie vanuit British-Indie onder het indentured-labourstelsel 1873-1916, Amrit, 1996
10. Sunil S. Amrit, *Migration and Diaspora in Modern Asia,* Cambridge University Press, 2011
11. Ibid.
12. R. Bhagwanbali, op. cit.
13. Carter, op. cit.
14. Walton Lai, op. cit.
15. Maithilisharan Gupt, Kisan Sahitya Sadan, Jhansi, 1916 (The third chapter of this book "Songs of Abolition: Anti Indenture Campaign in early Twentieth Century India" from the reference list of this bookA Edited by P. Pratap Kumar, *Indian Disapora, Sociocultual and Religious Worlds,* Brill Academic Publications, 2015
16. J W Burton, *Our Indian Work in Fji,* Methodist Mission Press, 1909
17. Gillian, op.cit.
18. Gayutra Bahadur, *Coolie Women: The Odyssey of Indenture,* Hurst Company, 2013 (Secondary Source)
19. George Greyson, *Report on Colonial Immigration from Bengal Presidency, 1883*
20. Gillain, op. cit.
21. www.girmit.org (Internet Source)
22. Dr. Kamlesh Sharma, *Ghulami: Slavery in Fiji, Indentured Labour Fiji,* Vivid Publishing,2016
23. Andrews & Greyson, *Indian Indentured Labour in Fiji,* Colourtype Press, Perth,1918
24. Ved Prakash Batuk, "Protest Songs of East Indians in West Guyana", The Journal of American Folklore, Vol. 77, No. 305, 1964, pp. 220-235
25. Ashutosh Kumar, *Coolies of the Empire,* Cambridge University Press, 2017
26. Gayutra Bahadur, op. cit.
27. Ibid.
28. Rajendra Prasad, *Tears in Paradise: Sufferings and Struggles of Indians in Fiji, 1879-2004,* Glade Publishers,2004 (Secondary Source, primary source unknown)

29. Greyson, ibid.
30. Tinker, ibid.
31. Brinsley Samaroo and David Dabydeen, *Indians in The Caribbean 'The Indian Connection': the influence of Indian Thought and Ideas on East Indians in Caribbean*, Hansib Publishing Limited, Hertfordshire,1987 (Secondary Source, Primary source : J Kriplani and Others, Indian Centenary Review, 1945)
32. Ashwini Desai and Ghulam Wahid, Inside Indian Indenture: A South African Story, 1860-1914, ASHRC Press, 2020, Secondary Source
33. Gayutra Bahadur , Reference xviii
34. Ibid., Secondary Source
35. Ibid. , Secondary Source
36. John D Kelly, A Politics of Virtue: Hinduism, Sexuality and Countercolonial Discourse in Fiji, University Of Chicago Press, 1991
37. Verene and Shepherd, *Maharani's Misery*, University of West Indies Press, 2002
38. Gayutra Bahadur, ibid.
39. Totaram Sanidhya and Benarsi Das Chaturvedi, Fiji *Dweep mein Mere Ekees Varsh*, Rajput Anglo Oriental Press 1914
40. Carter, op. cit.
41. Batuk, op. Cit.
42. David Northop, *Indentured Labor in the Age of Imperialism*, 1834-1922, Cambridge University Press, 1995
43. Gayutra Bahadur, ibid. Secondary Source
44. David Northop (Source 43)
45. R Prasad, op. cit.
46. Ibid., Secondary Source
47. David Northop, op cit.
48. Verene, op. cit.
49. Walter Lai, op. cit.
50. Greyson, op. cit.
51. R Prasad, op. cit.
52. Totaram op. cit.
53. Ashutosh Kumar, "Feeding the Girmitiya," *Gastronomica: Journal of Critical Food Studies*, Vol. 16, No. 1, Spring 2016, pp. 41-52
54. Tinker , op. cit.
55. R Prasad op. cit.
56. Verene, op. cit.
57. Kamlesh Sharma , op. cit.
58. Munshi Rehman Khan, Jeevan Prakash, Paramaribo, Suriname, 1943
59. Gayutra, op. cit.
60. David Northrop , op. cit.
61. Gayutra, op. cit.
62. Same, op. cit., Secondary Source
63. Totaram op. cit.
64. Ibid.
65. Carter, ibid.
66. Gayutra, op. cit.
67. Totaram , op. cit.
68. Ibid.

Reunion and Seychelles

"Why do you call me a coolie when I was born in the land of Saints"
(A song in British Guyana)[1]

Fugitive Coolie

1864, St. Dennis Court, Reunion

"My Lord, please save me or my master will kill me," pleads a half-clad dark person as he enters the courtroom. He has a sturdy iron chain tied around his neck.

"Who has tied this chain around your neck?", asks the judge.

"The priest, Sir."

"The priest? What nonsense! Why would the priest do such a thing?"

"Sir, my master beat me a lot in his presence and then both of them tied this chain around my neck like a dog."

The judge ordered the police to bring the evidence.

"Your majesty! This person is a fugitive, and that is why he has been chained. He has run away many times before. We had arrested him once before and granted the punishment of a hundred days of intense labor. Then, he was sent back to the plantation. Now he had again run away from there." The police sergeant gave this statement.

"Is it true?" The judge asked the coolie.

"Yes, my lord! My master beats me every day. I have pleaded at all forums, but I received no help. Now, I have come to you."

"Investigate the violence done on this person and if it is found to be true take action against the plantation owner accordingly.", directed the judge to the police.

This case ran for almost a year and finally the plantation owner was punished for one month of imprisonment.

(Based on an original case)[2]

First Consignment from South India

'Coolie' is a Tamil word meaning 'money in exchange of work'. Quite logical, but by that definition we all are coolies. It is believed that the Portuguese first used this term to refer to workers at the Coromandel coast and then the other Europeans also began using it. This word was used for those who did menial jobs. The word 'coolie' would remain the identity of *Girmitiyas* for many years to come. Whether they got an education, or a position of repute, they and their future generations might be called a 'coolie'.[3]

Indians were not the first coolies. The Chinese were being taken as labor to foreign lands even before the Indians, especially to South America. There are a large number of people of Chinese origin in Peru. I have already discussed that even in those times, China and India were the two most populated countries. If someone wanted to take ships full of workers, these were the places for it. Even now, people from these countries are working for the capitalists in one or other ways.

Chinese workers shall be discussed in this book but for now let's talk about Indians.

What is surprising is that from India it wasn't the British, but the French who first began to transport the coolies, and that too practically stealing them under British eyes. Between 1826 and 1830 France stole about 3000 workers from India and sent them to the Reunion Island, a small and beautiful island between Maldives and Madagascar.

Once upon a time Reunion Island was France's major sugar hub. In the latter half of the 19th century, sugar production considerably diminished. France began to focus more on their other colony Madagascar because of more fertile soil there. Standing on volcanoes, the Reunion Island is still one of the most picturesque islands and is called the 'Hawaii Island' of France.

Transporting indentured workers to the Reunion Island had probably started in the latter half of the 17th century, when some slaves were taken from Goa to the Reunion Island, but this fact cannot be ascertained.[4] It is, however true that Indian *Girmitiya*• reached Reunion Island much before they reached anywhere else. Around 1830 itself about 40,000 *Girmitiya* were found on this island. The French kept bringing stolen workers here and Britain didn't even get a whiff of it. When after two or three decades this theft came to light, France offered a deal. An agreement (The Franco-British Convention of 1860) allowed upto 6000 workers to be transported in a year. If one goes by the law of averages the French must have brought about 0.2 million people to the island. Till 1855, about 60,000 people had come from India while the total population of island was about 100,000. The actual numbers could be even greater. For instance, in just the Martinique area of the island, there were about 25000 Indians in 1884.[5]

This is a staggering figure. What were so many people supposed to do on a small island? Possibly two-third of them died due to the torturous labor they had to do there. Many jumped into the sea due to depression with no hope of a reunion with their loved ones. It is still prohibited to swim in the ocean at the Reunion Island because dangerous sharks lurk in its waters. Its possible that some Indians fell prey to them. But this is just a conjecture. Actual cause of so many deaths must have been the same as it was on the other islands.

In one French ship *Auguste* which had sailed from Puducherry, many sick workers were thrown off the ship to prevent the spread of the disease. Most of the workers were regularly beaten by their masters. Rape of the women workers were common and many were punished by denying them food and water.[6]

We must also take in account that the tradition of slavery hadn't been abolished in France. It means that people from India were coming

• The word "Girmitiya" was never used for people coming to this island in an established way, but the writer has used the word in place of "contract workers" or "coolies" at several places in the book. This has been done for the ease of writing and paraphrase.

at the same time when African slaves were bring brought. It is possible that many of these slaves could have been unsalaried or brought for meagre salary, but this fact hasn't been recorded in history factually. However, it is obvious that getting slaves from the India was easy.[7-8]

My assumption is that there must have been some powerful merchants from Madras province who helped sending the slaves forcibly or by luring them with an attractive deal. I couldn't find any mention of *Arkaati* agents for Reunion Island. Mostly in these French colonies, the workers were of Tamil origin brought via Puducherry. The plantation owners were responsible for their lodging and boarding.

In French colonies as compared to the British colonies, the system was less organized. In the beginning, the plantation owners not only tortured the workers but also withheld their salaries. This certainly annoyed the *girmitiya*. The island was the first place where *Girmitiyas* formed their labour union and fought for their rights in an organized manner. The plantation owners felt threatened by this. They spread the rumor among the French officials that these Indian workers would ruin their island. Their union was banned in 1837.[9]

But as per my analysis (there are facts too supporting this) that the *girmityas* here were always the ones fighting for their conditions of work. When some of them were sent to another island, they were reluctant to do more work for less money. I shall discuss this later. Though their union was banned on Reunion Island, they didn't give up. If they faced some oppression, they would switch from one plantation to another. The owner of the other plantations safeguarded them because they needed workers for their plantation. This was also the only island where Indians were adamant and living on their own terms. The natives here believed that the Chinese workers were simpler as compared to the Indians. This is a strange fact in *Girmitiya* history. On all other islands, Indians lived a suppressed life and the Chinese lived on their own terms, but here the situation was quite the opposite. I think this could be the difference between the culture of North India and South India. In Reunion Island there were more South Indians and at other places there were more North Indians.

Due to the civil resistance of these *Girmitiyas*, a law was passed in 1843 that if the plantation owner was reluctant to paying wages, the contract would be nullified. (Decree of 10 November,1843)

Reunion Island had a smaller number of female workers. But the *Girmitiyas* here found a strange solution for that too – polyandry! Often four or five men would be in a relationship with one woman. Sometimes this system would not work in a perfectly smooth manner and there would be many conflicts. Many murders happened due to this hostility.[10]

Present-Day Reunion Island

As per the 2017 census, 0.2 million people out of the total 0.8 million population are of Indian origin, meaning 25 % of the total population. It is a huge number. Jean-Paul Virapoullé is a contemporary leader of the Reunion Island and a member of parliament. His grandfather was brought long back as an indentured worker from Tamil Nadu.[11]

People of South Indian origin (mainly Tamil and Telugu) came to be known as *Malabar* on Reunion. Many people of Malabar origin can be found in Maldives too. Mrs. Nadiya Ramasamy of this origin is a major political leader of the island. These people are also called *Tamool* because they are of Tamil origin. They are mainly Hindus or atleast had been Hindus once.

Many Muslims too came here from North India, especially from Gujarat. They were called *Jarabe*. Many among them spoke Hindi or Gujarati. There were several Bhojpuri-speaking people too from United Province (now Uttar Pradesh). However, North Indians also came to be known as Malabari, usually due to marriages in Malabari families. *Malabar* and *Jarabe* are more like a religious demarcation. A few Hindu jewelers of Patiyar sub-caste also settled here in the 19th century, but they were prosperous people unlike *Girmitiya* laborers.[12]

Now among the 0.2 million Indians, Hindus are a small number, about 6-7 %. But it is gradually growing. Many were Muslims originally and many became Catholic Christians forcibly or voluntarily. One reason that I could think of is that the Hindus who came initially were lower caste people and their rituals were different than Brahmins. In India, they were prohibited from visiting temples, and knew little about religion. It was prohibited to make a Hindu temple on the Reunion Island for many years. Everybody had to go to the church. Later when temples were built, they were labelled pagan by the Christians. But what is strange that many Christians here follow Hindu rituals, especially the Tamils.

Today, Hindu religion is being propagated by several Tamil organizations and ISKCON (International Society for Krishna Consciousness). It is also typical of this island that you will find people having French names like Alexis and Jean Marie visting the church as well the Hindu temple. The priests here say, "If you go for worship twice, God will look at you twice." Beside this they also worship the 'Black virgin' here. It is an amalgamation of the Hindu Goddess Kali and Virgin Mary.[13]

William Dalrymple, historian and writer wrote about his experience in the Reunion Island:

"Here a Chinese Tao, an Indian Muslim, a modern Catholic, one African exorcist-sorcerer and a Tamil Hindu can be found in one family."[14]

When I was going through all the pictures of Reunion Island, I found small deep red colored temples lining the road everywhere. They look like Hanuman temple. When I looked closely, I discovered these were the temples of Saint Expedite. Nowhere else in the world can these temples be found in such density. Folklore is that in 1931, Vatican sent some cargo to this island, but the details were lost on the way.[15] On some paper there was written- "Expedito." People started worshipping 'Expedite' ever since. Red-colored temples cropped up everywhere. Finding devotion in a stray piece of paper in itself denotes a typical Indianness. Now in Reunion Island the Hindus have started believing that this imaginary saint is an incarnation of Vishnu.

One more instance of the amalgamation of Catholics and Hindus is the *Shraddh* (death ritual). The Hindus here first take the dead body to the church and then bring it to the Hindu priest. It is followed by performing the sixteen-day long *Shraddh* ceremony.

But the hurdles in communal harmony are not completely absent. There are examples of conflict between Hindus and the French Creoles. A few years ago, the Hindu temple of Herrumbre was demolished. This was a historical temple and established by the *Girmitiyas* who came here possibly in 1870. To my knowledge, there are not many people left on this island who have Hindu names. The president of the organization of people of Indian origin Paul Kanagi also has a French name. In fact, the French had made a rule from the very beginning to dissociate these workers from the Indian mainland. There papers were burnt. They were never taught to read or write in Indian languages. Their recollections were destroyed. Though many old women here could tell the story of the Ramayana in bits and pieces, they don't know the full meaning. The French-speaking Hindu priests here also know little about Indian culture.

These Indians got French citizenships only after 1920.[16] Before that, they were just immigrant foreign workers. Hence their rights were few. But after this, they began to get prosperous. Gilbert Kanabadi Motiyan is a Malabar of Tamil origin and one of the richest people on the island today. He owns an entire city Domain Mount Capri which has many showrooms and shops. His film *Indians from Mount Capri Estate* reveals many such secrets as to how his grandfather was brought as a worker for sugarcane fields. He says that his middle name *Kanabadi* was given by his father which could even actually be Hindu elephant god Ganapati. Gilbert goes every year to bow his head at temples in India. He never fails to remember the land of his ancestors. In his film when he stands in front of a deity the entire history of the *Girmitiyas* can be seen in his eyes. As if a *Girmitiya* has returned home after many years.[17]

This island has about twenty priests whose ordination was done by Tamil priests brought from Mauritius. The Tamil festival *Kavadi* is celebrated every year at the St. Andre Island here. A procession of Tamil deity Murugan is taken out and it is quite a fun fare. People of all religions celebrate it like a festival of the island. The birth of Lord Ganesha is celebrated by the name of *Sadurti*. Mahavishnu's festival *Yagardesi*, festival of the moon *Ponemi* and the festival of ancestors

Amavaasi are also celebrated now. Eid is also celebrated well here which people of *Jarabe* origin organize. *Diwali* and *Navratri* are also celebrated now. Especially, *Diwali* celebrations at Colossus Park and the *Desi Mela* here are quite popular. Many artists from India are invited to the Reunion Island on this occasion. Now even Bollywood is getting popular. The good old Hindi film song *"Mann dolay mera tan dolay"* (My heart sways, my body sways) is quite popular.

Many schools and university in Reunion Island teach Tamil. This is a positive beginning. For many years, Tamil was almost erased from this island and only French Creole was being used. A popular dish here is rice-curry. In the curry, Indian spices like turmeric powder, ginger, garlic, and cloves are used. The cuisine of Reunion Island is an amalgamation of Indian, Chinese, Arabian, and French cuisine.

The people here know that they can't return to their roots, but they are watering them, and new shoots are appearing. Indians don't need a visa to go to this island. They can live here for a fortnight without any visa. Reunion Island was in headlines when some remains of a Boeing-370 gone missing from Malaysia were found here. Some vestiges of our Indian culture are also found in Reunion Island.

Seychelles Island, Indian Ocean

Wavell John Charles Ramkalawan appears to be of African descent in his photograph. But his name Ramkalawan arouses some suspicion that he may be of Indian origin. Apparently, his great-grandfather came from Uttar Pradesh, first to Mauritius and then to Seychelles. Wavell Ramkalawan is a prominent politician in Seychelles and a Christian priest. He had also been a presidential candidate. But it is surprising to think about his great-grandfather. Under what circumstances would a labourer come here from Uttar Pradesh? How did he become a Christian? And how did he come to have relations with Africans?[18]

It is believed that thousands of years ago there was a Gondwana landmass. Perhaps a portion of it drifted away to form an archipelago of 115 islands in the Indian Ocean called Seychelles. Most of these islands are uninhabited. Just like India these islands were also discovered by

Vasco Da Gama in 1502. The first colonist to arrive here were the French comprising 15 White men, eight Africans and five Indians aboard the ship *Thelemaque*. This island was ruled by the French and the British alternatively, but in 1814 after Napoleon's defeat it came under British control.

The French began to bring slaves here since 1770 from South India. There are no specific details about the early ships which came here. In 1905 a ship named *Etruria* brought 135 labourers here from Madras. The chief crop here was sugarcane. But I could not find any records of *Girmitiya* life here or their barracks.

I did make some estimates though. Most Indians here are of South Indian origin. Many Christians are there with their last name ending in Reddy. Most of them are now concentrated in the Mahé Island of Seychelles. Maybe this is where they came to work, or they might have come here after finishing their *Girmitiya* life in Mauritius. Indians of Seychelles have fully assimilated here. They married Chinese and African people here and many converted to Christianity.

The total population of this island is 81,000 (2017), out of which 5000 are Indians. Technically now only about 6% people are Indians but about 80% people have Indian blood. This comes across as an amazing fact. Such a vast Indian heredity on a strange island! In whatever form it maybe it does make its mark. At last Indian culture is making a comeback. Hinduism is still the second largest religion here.

In the last three decades, Tamil Hindus have initiated the renaissance of their Indian culture. The Arul Minu Navasakthi Vinayagar Temple was built here and even the festival *Kavadi* is now celebrated. Hindus have declared it a holiday.

While researching about Mauritius and Seychelles Islands, a question came to my mind, which also holds good for other islands as well. After all the African slaves arrived first on all these islands and lived here for very long but their African culture perished here. Whereas on the other hand, the Indianness of Indians remained intact. How is it so?

The plausible reason for this seems to be that in India religion has a huge influence and the faith related to it has passed on from one generation to another. Africans came from different tribes and indigenous groups and didn't have a composite culture, whereas Indians, though coming from various states, were from Hindu and Muslim culture only. India, despite being diverse, was basically culturally unified. Additionally, Indians also mostly married to people of their own country, however Africans were more liberal in this regard.[19]

Also, similarity in their languages, living in same barrack, and having one feudal history could be other reasons. Africans were brought as slaves and once independent they wanted to break away from the shackles of their unhappy past. Indians, on the other hand, had come on their own accord. They did not hate their past as much as maybe the Africans did. One more factor can be that the Africans were brought when they were immature and hence weren't much aware of their culture. So much so that the Africans were even given names by the French and the British, such as Jacob or Chris. Indians there, however, kept the tradition of giving Indian names. These could be some of the factors why African culture perished and the Indian culture thrived.

References

1. Ved Prakash Batuk, Protest Songs ofEast Indians in West Guyana, The Journal of American Folklore, Vol. 77, No, 305, 1964, Page No,220-235 (Translated by the author from English)
2. Alesandro Stansiyani, Labor,Rights and Immigration, A comparison between Mauritius and Reunion, 1840-1880, Le movement Social, 2012 (Secondary source)
3. Gayutra Bahadur, Coolie Women: The Odyssey of Indenture, Hurst Company, 2013
4. Report of the High-level committee on Indian Diaspora, Ministry of Foreign Affairs, Chapter 6: Reunion
5. Same as ref. 4
6. Herbert Gerbeu, Engagees and Coolies on Reunion Island, Slavery's masks and Freedom's Constraints, (Colonialism and Migration Edited by Peter C Emmer) Doedrekht, 1986
7. Alesandro Stanziyani, Sailors, Slaves and Immigrants: Bondage in The Indian Ocean World, 1750-1914, Palgrave-Macmillan, 2014
8. Alesandro Stanziyani, Bondage, Labor and rights in Eurasia from Sixth to early Twentieth century, Bardhan Books, 2014
9. Sudel Fuma,L'esclavagisme a la reunion - 1797-1848, Diverse Ocean Indian, 1993
10. Marina Carter, Voices from Indenture, Experiences of Indian migrants in The British Empire, Leicester University Press, 1966
11. Senate France Website (Internet source)

12. S Jayasurya and Richard Pankhurst, The African Diaspora in Indian Ocean, Africa World Press, 2003
13. Le Promise, documentary directed by Gerald Periyar
14. William Dalrymple, The Age of Kali, Flamingo Publishers, 1998
15. Same as ref. 14
16. Report, ref. 4
17. Le Memoir Das Kanabadi, Documentary directed by Louis Vulcan
18. Appeal in Constitutional Court by Wavel John Charles Ramkalawan (Internet source)
19. Burton Benedict, Slavery and Indenture in Mauritius and Seychelles (From the book *Asian and African System of Slavery* Ed. by James L Watson, Cambridge University Press, 1980

Mauritius

From the dripping roof of the past
my present
drips plop, plop
In the soleless vessel
Of the future

- Abhimanyu Anat, Poet of Mauritius•

Jhunmun Gosain and Ganga Lake

"I dreamt that the Ganga has come to Mauritius, and there is a lake atop the mountain connected to the *Jahnvi* (River Ganges)."

It is difficult to ascertain the veracity behind this dream of Jhunmun Gosain. Some say one mysterious *Langlois* baba had guided him. I investigated story behind this baba.

One Pandit Sanjibanlal ji went to the Reunion Island as a *Girmitya* worker. He later migrated to Mauritius and purchased Langlois Saheb's (an Englishman) bungalow and settled down there. Since then, he came to be known as *Langlois* Baba and Jhunmun Gosain became his follower.

Jhunmun himself had run away from Sikarhata village in the Aara (Shahbad) district to Calcutta at the age of 14. In 1860, he came to Mauritius as a *girmitiya.* After his *Girmitiya* tenure, Jhunmun opened a shop in Mauritius and settled down there. He must have met *Langlois* Baba during this period.

• Internet, *Kavita Kosh.* Translated from Original in Hindi.

After seeing the dream that Ganges had flown down to Mauritius, he set out to look for it. After walking for several days amidst a volcanic crater on top of a mountain he at last found a lake which, as per his dream, was connected to river Ganges. He got erected a temple of Lord Shiva here. A statue of *Bhairon Baba* (Hindu Lord Shiva) was also brought here and installed.

After a few years, a *pandit* by the name of Tilakdhari asserted his claim on the temple. Tilakdhari was probably a Brahmin and Jhunmun Gosain may have been a Baniya. Tilakdhari thus had a stronger claim he felt. At last, Jhunmun Gosain had to make a separate temple for him there.

This lake named 'Ganga Lake' became popular and pilgrims began to throng here from all parts of the world. In 1973 water taken from the Ganges was poured into it. Now at the gate of this lake there is a 108 feet tall statue of *Mangal Mahadev*.

Jhunmun Gosain passed away in 1914, but before dying, he brought the Ganges to Mauritius![1]

Girmitiya Landowners

Sundarpur was a tiny village in district Patna (now district Bikram). About 150 years ago, a young *Kurmi* (a lower caste) lad Shivudhari Bhagat, came to the city in search of a job and never returned. Today, this *Kurmi*- dominated village belongs to the Pataliputra Vidhan Sabha constituency.

When Shivudhari Bhagat came to Mauritius in 1855, about 150,000 *Girmitiyas* had already arrived here. But nobody had ever imagined that this 28-year-old young man would initiate something that would change their lives.

Shivudhari finished his *Girmitiya* contract of three years and opened a shop in Mauritius along with two of his Indian friends. He began to buy small land plots and gradually amassed a huge land. This process of buying small plots of land and becoming the owner of a large landmass is known as "Grand Morcellment".

Besides turning the land into sugarcane plantations, he also divided it into small plots and built some Indian establishments there. For instance, in 1875 he bought 312 arpent (acres) of land and planned to sell one acre each at one hundred and fifty dollars. When sales picked up, the price rose to 200 dollars per acre. Farmers would live there and grow sugarcane in these small fields. I could not ascertain if this was some sort of cooperative farming. But at that time, big landowners and entrepreneurs like Shivudhari were very few. Later, many *Girmitiyas* adopted this model.

When I visit Sundarpur village today, I feel Shivudhari had acquired a bigger landmass than this entire village in Mauritius. Not many have heard of Sundarpur village in India, but Shivudhari's 'Plaines Wilhems' area is well known in Mauritius.

It was one success story how a bonded Girmitiya worker became a landowner/*Zamindaar* in a foreign land.[2]

Immigrant Ghat

9 September 1834, Calcutta

The Arkati had brought 36 people to Calcutta. They were all dark and strong built with unkempt hair. Some looked around vaguely while some sat with their heads down.

"What is their caste?"

"They are *Dhangars, my lord.*"

"What caste is that?"

"They are tribals from the Chhota Nagpur area -- *Uranv, Munda* people."

"Then it is okay. They are not Brahmin, or Khatri I hope?"

One well-dressed supervisor made them all stand together and asked them, "Are you all ready to go to Mauritius Island?"

"Where is this island?"one of them asked.

"Its near Calcutta in the middle of sea."

"How much money will we get?"

"Much more than in Assam or Bengal. *Mareech* Island has plenty of money. Wherever you dig, there is gold."

"Okay, we will go then *Saheb*. Where do we put our thumb impression?"

While the French were taking *Girmitiyas* to Reunion in 1826, the British began to take *Girmitiyas* to the neighbouring Mauritius in 1829. Both might have followed similar sea routes. What is surprising is that the British officers didn't discover these French smugglers to Reunion till thirty years!

Labourers of the Bihar and United Province referred to Mauritius as *Mareech*. Between 1824 and 1910, about 1,84,000 workers from Bihar were sent to Mauritius. This was about 40% of the total bonded labour there. Most people were from Gaya and Chhapra district, but many people were also from Bhojpur, Gopalganj and Champaran. Now let's look at history of indentured labour in Mauritius in a chronological manner.

After being abandoned by the Dutch, the island became a French colony in 1721 and they began bringing laborers here. As per earliest document, in 1728 the Governor of this island Ile de France went to Pondicherry and brought 135 unpaid slaves and 95 paid contract labourers.[3] Slaves were usually under eighteen years of age whereas labourers were above eighteen. I suspect that slaves may have been children abducted by force or threat. Later, many plantation owners bought slaves and workers. In 1792 from the port of Calicut, each ship brought about three hundred slaves each.[4] These mentions of slavery sound true because till then the tradition of slavery hadn't been abolished. Till 1806 about 6162 Indians had reached Mauritius.[5] One figure of the French rule in Mauritius says that about 20,000 people had come to this island.[6] Workers who came in that period were *Telinga* (Telugu), *Malabar*i (Tamil), and Bengali. What condition these slaves lived in, can be ascertained from the punishments they got. If they ran away once, one of their ears was chopped off, if they ran away again the remaining ear was chopped off, and third time they were shot![7]

I found it difficult to retrieve details of people brought in during the French rule. Firstly, all the archives are in French and secondly no books have their apt descriptions. Yet this much can be deduced that just like Reunion Island, French imposed their language, religion and culture on them. I assume that Indians might have got converted to Christianity and lost contact with India.

When Britishers were fighting to gain control on this island, the French put these Indians on front. From 1748 to 1810 many well-built people were brought from India and an army was created.[8] Ultimately, the British won, and they got control over this island in 1815. The slave Indians of French Mauritius were lost but the slaves of British Mauritius were not like them.[9] They cherished their Indianness for decades to come. They came in large numbers and ultimately dominated the entire island.

After the British occupancy in 1815, Governor Farquhar brought 835 prisoners from Bihar and rest of Bengal province. They were made to construct roads in Mauritius. Till 1828 they had brought 1028 prisoners. They were kept in prisoners' camps as slaves. In 1838, the prisoners above 65 years of age were set free.[10-11]

Meanwhile, in 1825, the British made the sugar import from Mauritius tax-free. This increased the production and sale of sugar. But it was getting tough without laborers. So, they decided to get labour from the Penang area of China and from Singapore, but these people couldn't bear the climate and fell sick. They were sent back. Then there were suggestions of getting labour from Africa, but it was struck down after the abolition of slavery. The British officers realized that manpower and subservience was nowhere more abundant than in India.

Then began the *Girmitiya* experiment which was called 'The great experiment'.

In 1831 Ms. William Mathieson from Calcutta brought 151 laborers from Bihar to the island. They worked in the sugarcane fields of Rivière du Rempart area of John Sampson. The date that is more famous is 2 November 1834 when 36 Bihari laborers came aboard the ship *Atlas* to Port Louis in Mauritious and worked in the sugarcane plantation owned by a Scottish man named Arbuthnott. 2 November is still a holiday in Mauritius to commemorate those 36 Girmitiya laborers who had come here. In another ship the same year, more people from Bihar arrived. There are records of 35-year-old Gangadin, 30-year-old Hardayal and

24-year-old Munni who came here. Gangadin worked in the sugarcane fields till he passed away at the age of 90.

Between 1856 and 1869, some freed slaves from Mozambique (Africa) were also brought in. But the system of bringing in Indian laborers was more organized and permanent. As a result, 95% of *Girmitiyas* were Indians.

Initially nobody was ready to come to Mauritius, calling it a *Kaala Paani* (Black Waters). The Britishers thought of many devious ways to bring them to Mauritius. For instance, District Collectors were asked to reduce the distribution of grain in their district to half so that people were forced to flee. Yet people were not ready to go. They were made to agree by giving them several incentives.

Even in this shorter journey, deaths were common in early days. In 1858, ships from Calcutta reported 19 deaths per thousand, and ships from Madras, about 5 per thousand. This difference could be because of frequent outbreaks of communicable diseases like cholera and typhoid in Calcutta.[12]

In 1910 when the *Girmitiya* era ended, 4,51,000 Indians were living in Mauritius.[13]

Labour in Mauritius

When labourers were brought to Mauritius they were kept in the huts of older slaves, which soon turned into an Indian village. In fact, they established a *Panchayat* (village administration) of their own which they called *baithaka*. In this *baithaka* they resolved their mutual disputes. Later they began making their own religious bodies, like the Muslims created their *Jamaat*.[14]

In 1835, two harsh ordinances came into existence.

According to ordinance 10-

"If any labourer or an apprentice commits a crime or doesn't work according to the contract (not working, not showing up for work, not completing the work properly), he/she could be subjected to three months of imprisonment or a fine of five pounds."

According to ordinance 16-

"If three or more than three labourers joined hands for demands like changing contract or raising wages and hence obstructing work, they could be imprisoned for up to six months."

Thus, their wings were clipped in the beginning itself. In 1847 came the 'double-cut law', according to which if a labourer was absent for more than six days in a month then he would not get wages for the entire month.[15]

These ordinances were fiercely opposed by liberals in London, but the governor of Mauritius explained that these ordinances were for the betterment of the empire and discipline in production. According to them, these were not related to slavery. But how could the illiterate Indian labourers understand these ordinances? They would often break these rules and consequently punished and tortured. When in 1922, these ordinances were finally abolished, these poor people had already been exploited for eight decades.

At Port Louis in Mauritius these lines are etched at the Aapravasi Ghat, the former immigration depot for indentured labour from India:

"For whom history left no evidence
Whose complete story history didn't tell
Those who irrigated this soil with their sweat
And turned stones into ample fields of gold
First Girmitiya was the son of this soil
He was ours, yours and of all of us."

Casteism in Mauritius

Girmitiyas sent to Mauritius belonged to different castes but majority of them were from lower castes. I had thought that *Mahadalit* (extremely lower castes) could be here in majority, but research shows otherwise. As per the figures from 1813[16]:

1. Upper caste *Brahmins* and *Kshatriyas*- 19%
2. *Vaishya*, *Ahir* and other middle castes- 36%
3. *Dalits* (mainly *Chamars)*- 23%

4. Muslims- 19%
5. Others- 3%

19% of *Girmitya* labourers were from upper caste! They must have been financially weak to take such a step as to cross *kala pani.* In 1904, one Brahmin Gajadhar had returned to his village after earning well from Mauritius, but he had to pay 200,000 rupees as fine to his village Panchayat, to get his caste back. The villager's logic was that on the ship, they ate contaminated food shared with lower castes, didn't bath, and pray properly, and thus lost their Brahminhood. There is a story about a Brahmin voyager who was forcibly made to eat fish.[17]

I got to know that caste system is now non-existent among the Hindus of Mauritius. They can now marry among themselves without considering them as inter-caste unions. Maybe because there was just one social strata- *Girmitiya.* But a kind of casteism did take root in Mauritius. After spending some years on sugarcane fields, some labourers would become *Sardar* (leader). They were better paid, and this was the beginning of a socio-economic stratum.

Broadly, there are two categories of Hindus in Mauritius. One is the *Grand Nasyon* or the upper caste group. The second is the *Ti Nasyon,* which is the lower caste community. Amongst the upper castes there are three castes- --*Maharaj* or *Maraj (Brahmins), Babuji (Kshatriya),* and *Vaish (Vaishya).* There are a few other sub-castes. For instance, *Khatri* are a kind of *Babuji* caste. *Ahir, Kurmi* and *Koiri* belong to the *Vaish* community. *Chamar, Noniya* and *Dusadh* belong to the *Dalit* (lower caste) community. Tribal people who had come from Orissa and present day Jharkhand are called "*Junglee*" (wild). Chinese is also considered a caste.

Mauritius of today has *Vaish Mukti Sangh* (trader caste union) and *Gehlot Rajput Mahasabha* (warrior caste union). The lower-caste *Chamar* followers of *Arya Samaj* made *Arya Ravived Pracharini.* However, talking about casteism in Mauritius may get one into trouble. In the French magazine *Le'Express* of 9th January 2010 when an article was published about casteism in Mauritius, copies of the magazine were burnt by the "Front Commune Hindu" organisation in protest.[18]

If one observes closely, there is a glimpse of regionalism too. Most of the fields in the Belle Mare area have been bought by people from Aara district in Bihar.[19] It is possible that in the initial days these people coming from nearby villages made some kind of regional ghetto, which got diluted over time.

Women Seafarers of Mauritius

In the early ships, women were almost absent. By 1842 only about 1% were women.[20] With such a small number of women, men would have been hugely competitive leading to conflicts. May be this was the reason why women's quota of indentured labour was increased. By 1884 women's percentage had reached above 50% of the total.[21] What must also be noted is that marriages from India were illegal here. The couple had to get it registered again in Mauritius, which very few people did and it led to a lot of legal conflicts later.

There are reports of sexual exploitation during the voyage, for example one Dr. R Brown was accused of forcibly undressing a *Girmitiya* women under the influence of liquor. Later he was punished.[22]

Girmitiya women used to wear a lot of gold jewellery, which was their *solah shringaar* (sixteen adornments). Just as male *Girmitiyas* would buy property after saving money, the women would buy gold. Gifting their wives gold ornaments, especially pendants made of *Girni* (Guinea coins) was common. These were 17th century coins made of gold imported from the Guinea (West Africa) and minted in Britain. Later these coins ceased to circulate as currency and began to be fashioned into jewelery by Port Louis jewellers. Women would wear them to marriages and other occasions. It was also common for these coins being given as gift by grandmothers to their grandchildren. Later the new generation began to melt these *Girnis* to make new jewellery. Although the white men would call this waste of money, these coins became a symbol of Indian prosperity.

Indian Culture and Religion

The condition of Indians in Mauritius was better than Reunion Island as they could preserve their Indian culture. *Girmitiyas* came from

Bihar, Orissa, Maharashtra, Tamil Nadu and Andhra, and there were businessmen from Gujarat and Sindh came as well. As per the 2017 census, out of the 1.2 million population, 0.8 million are of Indian origin. Men labourers from China also married Indian women, with their children carrying Indian genes.

The schools in Mauritius have a three-language policy. French and English are compulsory. Hindi and Urdu are popular as third language. Many children in Mauritius can read and write Hindi. In an old census of 1960, about 60% Indians reported their language to be Hindi or an Indian language but not French.[23]

In Mauritius you will still find Ramayana recitation along with hand-cymbals and women singing songs. *Mahashivratri* remains the most popular festival celebrated here with lots of pomp. It is celebrated for about four to nine days in the months of February-March. Besides this the festival of the Tamil god *Murugan* known as *Taipusam* is also popular here. *Ganesh Chaturthi* is a national holiday. *Diwali* and *Holi* are festivals that even Christians celebrate along with Hindus. *Ugadi* and *Makar Sankranti* are also celebrated here.

Swami Krishnanand Sevashram has played a major role in the promotion of Hinduism in Mauritius. His Ayurveda Ashram was established in 1983, with about 200 in-patients and 400 out-patients a week. It is one of the largest Ayurveda ashrams of the world. Besides this ISKCON also has constructed temples, Arya Samaj and Swami Lakshmanacharya Vishva Shanti Foundation are also thriving in Mauritius. In recent years, *Hindu Swayamsewak Sangh* (a branch of Indian politico-religious front *Rashrtriya Swayamsevak Sangh)* have become active. After India and Nepal, the greatest number of Hindus are in Mauritius!

One reason of Indianness surviving in Mauritius is that people of Indian origin are prominent in politics. Other than Karl Hoffman, all presidents have been of Indian origin. Other than Paul Bérenger all Prime Ministers as well. Most of the Prime Ministers and Presidents of Mauritius have been from Bihar, obviously because they are in majority.

The first President of Mauritius Seewoosagur Ramgoolam was from *Harigaon* of district Bhojpur. His father Mohit Ramgoolam had been brought here at the age of 18, in 1896 on board the ship 'Hindoostan'. Seewoosagur Ramgoolam could find his ancestral village, but President Rashkishwar Puryag is still looking for his roots. His great-grandfather had come to Mauritius as a labourer from Bihar, while his brother's family stayed back. He could find that he is connected to the Wajitpur village in Punpun area of Patna but not his ancestral tree. Bihar's Chief Minister Nitish Kumar has connected his lineage to *Mahto toli* at *Masaudhi*, but nobody knows how true it is.[24]

References

1. Vishwanandan Govindan, Subjects of History: Gokula and Jhunmun Giri Gosain, Indentured migrants to Mauritius, Serial Publication, Main in India, 92(2), page 333-52
2. Richard Allen, Slaves, Freedom and Indentured labour in Colonial Mauritius, Cambridge University Press, 1999
3. Berton Bennedict, Slavery and Indenture in Mauritius and Seychelles (from James El Watson edited 'Asian and African system of Slavery'), University of California Press, 1980
4. Hughes Tinker, New System of Slavery, The export of Indian Labour Overseas, 1830-1920, Oxford University Press, London, 1974
5. Burton ref. 3
6. Richard ref. 2
7. Same ref. 2, Secondary source
8. Burton ref. 3
9. K. Hazari Singh, The History of Indians in Mauritius, Macmillan, 1975
10. Richard ref. 2
11. R.S. Kuchinsky, Demographic survey of the British Colonial Empire, Vol.2, Oxford University Press, 1949
12. Richard ref. 2
13. David Northop, Indentured Labour in the age of Imperialism 1834-1922, Cambridge University Press, 1995
14. Burton ref. 3
15. Same ref. 3
16. Same ref. 3
17. Mathieu Claveyrolas, The 'Land of the Vaish'? Caste Structure and Ideology in Mauritius, South Asia Multi-disciplinary Academic journal, Online Source, 27th May 2015
18. Same ref.17
19. Richard ref. 2
20. Burton ref. 3
21. Richard ref. 2
22. Verene A. Shepherd, Maharani's Misery: Narratives of a Passage from India, University of the West Indies Press,2002
23. Burton ref. 3
24. Giridhar Jha, 'Mauritius President Rashkishwar Puryag finds his ancestral roots in Bihar', Mail Today, 2 January, 2013

Fiji Island

Fiji Group of Islands, South Pacific Ocean

"With knife and spade I now spend my day and night
Green shoots of sugarcane know my heart's plight"

(A Bidesiya sung by some Girmitiya)[1]

The Girmitiya Puzzle

I read a report on Satish Rai, a documentary film maker from Sydney, whose grandparents had been *Girmitiyas* in Fiji. In 1994, Satish Rai came to India in search of his ancestors, knowing almost nothing about them except that they belonged to Basti District in Uttar Pradesh. Basti is a huge district, and it was almost like finding a needle in a haystack. People with surname *Rai* in that district were traditionally *Bhoomihar Brahmins*. But there were thousands of such *Bhoomihar Brahmin* families. Satish Rai did not give up and visited India continuously for almost for twenty years. Ultimately, he managed to find some clue and reached village Balrampur where he located someone from his clan, one Naeem Rai.

To his dismay Naeem Rai turned out to be a Muslim! But, their facial features had a striking resemblance. When Satish dug into his family history, he discovered that his grandmother was some rich Rai Bahadur's wife. For some unknown reason, she ran away from home. *Arkati* agents in those days were on the look out for such type of desperate women who did not have a place to go and must have lured her to go to Fiji. She on her part must have found their proposal attractive because she feared that Rai Bahadur would find her from any corner of India and bring her back. She met a man during the journey whom she later married.

Meanwhile, the Rai Bahadur ostracized her parent's family and thus their family converted to Islam. Naeem Rai is one of the grandsons of that family.[2]

Mahatma of Fiji

In 1893, a poor Brahmin Totaram Sanidhya reached Prayag in search of a job, where an *Ahir* (cowherd caste) gave him shelter. While wandering in Kotwali Chowk in Prayag, he met a stranger who offered him an attractive job. That's how an intelligent Brahmin was fooled by an *Arkati* agent.

When Totaram reached the depot, about a hundred men and sixty women were already sitting there. While they were cooking food, Totaram did not know even how to light a stove. *Arkati* assured him that the misery would end once he reaches Fiji.

He told, "It will be a heaven. You will be eating mangoes, gulping bananas, and sipping sugarcane juice in peace"

Totaram and others were taken to a magistrate. They were told beforehand to answer every question in the affirmative. Within barely twenty minutes, 165 people had put their thumbmarks on the agreement!! Totaram grew suspicious and refused to sign the papers. He gave the excuse that he had never done any physical labour and even showed them his soft palm. But, he was locked up in a solitary cell without food or water for a day. Ultimately, he accepted defeat and signed the papers to go to Fiji.

When he reached Fiji, he refused to work but was forcibly sent on a boat to a plantation. He began to work in the fields but could not bear it. He had never done farming in his life. Now he had to spade the field the whole day. It made him extremely tired and hungry. So, he asked the supervisors to increase his rations.

The White man asked him sarcastically, "Are you a horse or a man?"

He answered, "I was a man before, now this spade has made me a horse."

The Whites there even detested the breath of non-White Indians, saying that their breath would spread disease. This motivated Totaram to rebel against the miseries imposed by British empire. He began to write agonies of Fiji to Indian politicians, especially Mohandas Karamchand Gandhi. When he requested Gandhi to send an Indian barrister to Fiji, Gandhiji replied to his letter in Hindi. This was significant because Gandhi usually wrote in Gujarati or English. The letter is reproduced below:

Shravan day 8, Year 1967 (Hindu calendar)

"Received your letter. Knowing about the misery of my Indian brothers there makes me miserable. There is no opportunity to send a barrister from here. Please keep me informed about whatever situations arise. I shall convey this to England. I do understand your trouble. For this work, we would be needing an English-speaking nationalist man. If I come across someone I will send. I shall await your next letter. Regards from Mohandas Karamchand Gandhi."

Later Gandhi's advocate Manilal Doctor was sent to Fiji, which I shall discuss later.

Totaram made significant contributions to Indian culture and Hindu religion. He acted as a priest and often mentored the fellow *Girmitiyas*. He would advise them against conversion to Christianity. It was he who started *Ram Leela* festival in Fiji and invited several religious preachers over there. Totaram and his wife returned to India after spending 21 years there and began to live with Gandhi in Sabarmati Ashram. During this time, in the Madras session of the Congress in 1914, Totaram spoke as a representative of the Indians in Fiji. He went from village to village preaching against the *Girmitiya* tradition. Eventually, due to untiring effort of people like him, Girmitiya tradition was abolished in 1917. Due to these reasons, Totaram Sanidhya is known as the Mahatma Gandhi of Fiji.[3]

Island of Cannibals?

Fiji is a group of about 300 islands and 500 small landmasses. 110 of them are inhabited. Millions of years ago these islands were volcanoes, but they are extinct now. This island is also known as the 'Heaven of Pacific Ocean', where coco-palms sway in the breeze, and is abound with lush greenery and a superficial calmness. Superficial because many pains and many sufferings are hidden beneath. This is the land of the *Girmitiyas*. The *Kariya* hill on the Ba Island is a black hill where many Indians had their plantations and settlement.

Journey to Fiji was difficult, and many ships fell prey to the South Pacific Ocean. One of the first British ships that could reach belonged to Peter Dillon, an Indian man of Irish origin. He was the captain of the Royal Navy for Trafalgar and Calcutta.[4] In 1813 his ship *Hunter* under captain Robinson came to Fiji in search of sandalwood. When they reached here, they had a conflict with the tribal people of Fiji.

Dillon conspired with one local migrant named Charles Savage, to destroy a boat of Fiji natives. Dillon and Savage wanted to run away and get on to their ship 'Hunter', but they were unsuccessful. Dillon climbed with his people onto a hillock, but gradually thousands of *Valiya* natives surrounded the hillock. Charles Savage devised a plan to escape but Dillon announced that whoever tries to run away would be shot.[5] Charles Savage lived in Fiji for many years and spoke the local language fluently.[6] He said he would go down and make an offer of peace. Dillon asked to leave behind the guns. Savage came down but the deal couldn't happen. Contrary to that, these people killed and ate up Savage. What is ironic is that it was Savage who had once taught the Fiji islanders to shoot a gun, and his disciples ate him up![7]

Meanwhile, Dillon was vicious and made his move carefully. His people were already holding eight *Valiya* natives captive on his ship, one of them the brother of the head priest of the *Valiya* people. Dillon negotiated and The *Valiya* agreed. Meanwhile, several tribals had climbed the hillock but Dillon was pardoned. The hillock is now known as 'Dillon rock'. Some people contest this story saying that the natives of Fiji weren't cannibals. But the islands near Australia did have cannibals, Fiji being one of them.

The First *Girmitiyas* of Fiji

When British started sugarcane plantations in Fiji, local tribal people were not ready to work. So, laborers were brought from Solomon Islands (now Vanuatu) but they also ran away. At last local governor Sir Arthur Gordon contacted the 'recruitment agencies' in Calcutta. In 1879, 31 laborers from the French colony in Reunion Island were taken to an island 'New Caledonia' and from there the British took them over to Fiji. These laborers weren't naïve as they had spent many years as *Girmitiya*. They refused to work complaining of harsh conditions, and thus sent back. In 1881, 38 laborers were brought via same route and a few among those also returned. Some people were exhausted of the travel and hence decided to stay back, married Fijian women. They never had a 'reunion' with Reunion.[8]

Meanwhile on 14 May 1879, 463 laborers were brought from Calcutta on board the ship *Leonidas*, and this process continued for the next 40 years. Approximately 60,000 Indian laborers were brought here. In those days an ordinary ship would take 73 days to reach Fiji, but later steamer ships would reach in a month. One of them is particularly memorable in *Girmitiya* history.

In 1884, a ship named *Syria* left Calcutta with 479 laborers for Fiji. The ship was supposed to reach Fiji in about 58 days. The passengers were a motley group of enthusiastic laborers. At last, they spotted the Fiji Islands in the far horizon. But about four miles away from the island, the ship collided with the Nasilai reef resulting in a hole in the ship's bottom. The ship began sinking. Sir Gordon sent a rescue mission which saved some people. But 59 *Girmitiyas* drowned, shouting helplessly.[9]

The sinking of the *Syria* has been well captured in this Fijian poem below:

"Dark night, sensational wind, sails fluttered above
On the chest of Fiji, Syria moved further
In the outburst of the storm, Syria hit the rocks
On one side it began to sink, hurry-scurry among the people
Many seafarers drowned, sank to the bottom of the sea."[10]

When the labourers alighted from the ship, they were quarantined for about a month on the uninhabited Nukulau island. They were also made to undergo a medical-checkup and those found unfit were sent back to India. Those who were slightly unfit were given less work and less money till they got fully fit. People would try to escape this island as well. Two South Indians spotted Viti Lau Island from there and mistook it for India They jumped into the ocean to swim there but unfortunately drowned some distance away. After that no one attempted to escape by jumping into the see. Besides, they were well guarded by security personnel.[12]

From Nukulau Island the *Jahaji Bhais* (seafarer brothers) would be separated. Many would perhaps never meet again. *Sahebs* wearing helmets would push them into goods carriages and take them away. Some blood brothers would also be separated. Assuming that they would be living nearby to each other they did not even bid farewell to one other. Gurumurthi and his brother came on a ship from North Arcot in Andhra Pradesh in 1911. But in Fiji they were sent to separate islands. For the next 68 years, Gurumurthi kept looking for his brother but never found him. In 1979, Gurumurthi passed away. Not just brothers, many couples were separated too. Venkatva Reddy worked in the Nakawai Estate. He was separated from his wife. Deeply distressed, one day he took leave from the manager to go to hospital. He walked to Lautoka about 18 miles away and committed suicide by jumping into the sugar mill shredder there. Shreds of his body got stuck in the parts of the machine.[13]

In the same context, I would mention about a Muslim couple Laliya and Ismail. For five years, they kept searching for each other and finally when they got to know their whereabouts, the plantation owner didn't allow them to meet. Ismail was forcibly sent back to India. This grief killed Ismail as soon as he reached Calcutta. When Laliya came to know about his death, she was devastated. She was sick for many days but even in that condition her owners made her work every day. This tragic story of Laliya and Ismail has been recorded in Totaram's book, and it is quite possible that after reading such heart wrenching stories, the movement for abolishing the tradition of Girmitiya started in India.[14]

Coolie Lines

The largest firm in Fiji was the Australian company Colonial Sugar Refining (CSR) whose mills were established at Nausori in 1882, Labasa in 1884, and Lautoka in 1924. Another company, the Vancouver Sugar Company had a mill in Nauva which was later shut down.[15]

Girmitiyas were kept in barrack-like houses with rooms 10 feet long and 7 feet wide. There was no flooring, but they were plastered with cowdung to make a floor. The roof was covered with iron sheets. Each room on an average had three people. These barracks were known as *coolie lines*. In some pockets the conditions were slightly better. At Nausori, CSR Company had taps installed and there were also septic tanks attached to bathrooms. In general, Coolie Lines would generally be smelly and den of diseases. Whites would cross the place covering their noses.

There were no bathrooms. One had to go to the river for taking bath. Often there was only one tap shared by the workers, leading to conflicts every morning. *Sardars* would fill water first. Many people would be awake the whole night to fill water. The worst back-breaking work was to carry water in a drum to the field workers. *Bidesiya* was a popular song in Coolie Lines:

"The night doesn't pass, in this cell dark
Whom do I tell my pain O Bidesiya
Day & night my life passes in pain
My eyes have now gone dry O Bidesiya"[16]

Another one:

"All joys aren't in the CSR cell
6 feet wide and 8 feet long
Therein lies my spade, my livelihood
Therein my grinding stone and stove
Therein my firewood
That is my palace and my palace grand
That is my golden palace of dreams"

When they would come back at 4 pm after work, their hands and feet would be covered in blisters. Next day they couldn't even lift the spade, but the *Sardar* would beat them if they refused, and they would get no money as well. They would whip their backs calling them 'bloody bastard'. Many hanged themselves in despair and many drowned themselves in the river.

The time between 4 pm in the evening and 9 pm at night was spent in filling water and cooking food. And early morning at 3 am, the *Bhishti* would wake everyone up. Laborers would get busy cooking breakfast and by 9 am be back to the fields.

Wages were distributed every Friday evening at 8 pm. There would be long queues and huge arguments about money. They would return home at about 10 pm with some money. Saturday was half day and Sunday was a holiday. On Saturday evening, Coolie Lines would light up with singing and dancing. Someone irrespective of caste would become a Pandit and narrate a tale from the hindu epics like Ramayana or Mahabharata. Everyone would form a circle around him and listen quietly. Later, sweets were distributed, and they all feasted together.

When *Bidesiya* was sung, the whole atmosphere would turn sad. Women would cry. One *Bidesiya* was-

"I ran away from my land; all was left behind
Go die recruiter, you ruined my marital bed"

Recruiter here meant the *Arkati*.

Another *Bidesiya* is: -

"Who will listen to the misery of Jhinki, the Saheb beats me bad
Our Sardar is a complaint monger, and Ramdaiyya is hostile"

[*Jhinki* is saying here that *Saheb* beats her, Sardar forwards complaints and his friend Ramdaiyya has also turned a foe].[17]

Women would sing for *Kulambars*-

"We have been broken dead by this work O Ram
Still, you scold me O Bidesiya;
We nourish the garden with blood and sweet
Sitting you only pass orders O Bidesiya"

Later, there were also weekly markets where free *Girmitiyas* would set up temporary shops. Here laborers would go dressed up in whatever best clothes they had. Grains, pulses, corn etc. were sold. Muslims would sell *halal* goats. There were tailors mending wear and tear in clothers, and barbers giving haircuts sitting on the ground. Part-time fortune-tellers would be reading palms of people.

Kothiwale, *Kulambar* and fields

There were different categories of work. For instance, sowing sugarcane or weeding was comparatively easier. This was done in a fixed area by one labourer in a day. One full task consisted of weeding an area of 1300 x 600 feet in one day with a spade.[18] One would get the daily wage only after completing this task. Women also did the same work, but they had smaller areas to cover and were paid less, often three-fourths of what the men got. Though this task appears to be easy, conditions were harsh. If left incomplete, a penalty was imposed. Fields were tilled not only with bullock, but also with horses. This was a new experience for Indian labourers. Controlling the horses was far more difficult than controlling bullock.

If the work was too torturous, one could complain to the Inspector. But they visited only once or twice in a year. One could go to a court too, but courts were far away and going there required a 'pass'. Obviously, the plantation owners never granted pass. Often in such situations, labourers would beat up the *Sardar* and the *Kulambar* (overseer). When a gentleman like Totaram Sanadhya was punched several times by a White man, he also hit him back in retaliation bruising his lips. He kept pleading in English, but Totaram didn't understand what he was saying so he continued beating. When he stopped beating him, the White man told him not to speak about this incident to anyone. Getting beaten up by a coolie was demeaning for a White man. After this fight, the same White man offered his hand of friendship to Totaram ji."[19]

If arguments grew out of hand, the *kulambars* would take them to the court. They would often exaggerate the matter and blame the labourer solely. In 1907, 1461 labourers were taken to court, which was about 13% of the total bonded labour!

Cane knife was the only weapon the labourers had, which they would always keep it alongside them and even holding it while sleeping. Even today the Fiji families of Indian descent keep cane knives as souvenir of their *Girmitiya* history.

Walter Gill has written in his book[20]-

"Once a White kulambar was roaming in Coolie Lines and he saw a dog. He cut the dog with a cane knife into shreds and threw the pieces into a labourer's house. The labourer, a Muslim, was so enraged that he beheaded the white man with the same cane knife."

Kulambars were White men and *Sardars* were chosen from among the *Girmitiyas*. These sycophants Sardars were their spies too. A few *Sardars*, however, favored the labourers and were respected a lot by the *Girmitiyas*. Amongst the most dangerous *Kulambars* was Gor-Jones and among *Sardars* it was Ramgareeb and Nand Kishor. One *Brahmin Girmitiya,* Sevanandan, committed suicide due to the torture by Gor-Jones. Ironically, just before his suicide, Gor-Jones had released an order to make him a *Sardar*. When the tortures by Gor-Jones grew, there was an indictment against him, and he was fined – but just 3 pounds![21]

Tortures were common everywhere. Once a hospital attendant Barnicot threw boiling hot water on the private parts of a labourer named Poligardu and kept beating him till he fainted in anguish. Similarly, in 1912, another *Girmitiya* named Sewagram probably committed some small theft at Raravai estate. He was first beaten, arm-twisted, and then was forcibly made to drink kerosene.[22]

Women labourers would be tied naked to a tree and molested in front of their children. Whites would try to take advantage of beautiful women and if they refused, they and their husbands were beaten up. It was prohibited to bring children to the fields. One woman's child was running a fever, so she brought him along with her to the fields. She kept holding the child to her bosom while the White man kept whipping her. Seeing this another White man felt pity for her and came to her rescue. Whipping was a regular ritual. There was probably no *Girmitiya* who had never been whipped. If you did not wake up at 3 in the morning- whip, any waywardness in the fields –whip, break any rule – whip, if you laugh loudly – whip, if you cry --whip.[23]

At the Nusuwasau plantation, a woman Narayani gave birth to a baby on 16th August 1919, but the baby died after four days. The woman was still bleeding profusely but she was given the task of breaking rocks. She was unable to do this work, so *Sardar* Muniram requested *Kulambar* Blamfield to assign her some other work. Blamfield pulled Narayani's hair and banged her head on the stones several times. Then he hit her several times with a baton. The hospital was five miles away and *Girmitiya* Kaaliram carried her on his back. Dr. Hailey saw the patient and wrote, "She was brutally beaten to the extent beyond human imagination."[24] Blamfield asked *Sardar* Muniram to take the blame and paid him a bribe of two pounds. He also threatened him that if he didn't do so, he would shoot Kaaliram. But when the investigating officers strictly interrogated Muniram he told everything as it had happened. Blamfield was indicted. Narayani recorded her statement in the court on a stretcher. In spite all this, Blamfield was released. Narayani lost her mind after the trauma of the incident and was sent back to India.[25]

After the labourers were beaten, they didn't have any ointment or creams to apply to their wounds. Instead, they had found some wild leaves which they ground to a paste, and it worked fine as a medicine. Although this didn't help much because next day again, they got beaten. The Whites were also smart enough to beat them between Thursday and Saturday so that their wounds healed a bit over the weekend and Monday onwards they were again fit to work. But the weather was moist and warm, hence wounds wouldn't heal quickly. Some *Girmitiyas* who went towards the forests to fetch wild leaves never returned.

Gradually complaints began to reach the Governor but due to lack of evidence and witnesses, they would become ineffective. The 'Agent General of Immigration' had the responsibility of labour rights, and he did collect facts, but they were all dismissed. For example, a labourer's hand was amputated but saying it was an accident, the court acquitted the manager of the plantation.[26]

In other incidence, one labourer was beaten so badly that his ribs were broken, and he died due to internal hemorrhage. This enraged one of his fellow *Girmitiyas* and he attacked the *Kulambar* lethally with an axe. The labourer was given a punishment of 24 whiplashes and ten years of imprisonment, while *Kulambar* walked free.[27]

Girmitiya people also established an informal cooperative society, where they deposited money and used it to fight cases of oppression. But this fund wasn't enough as compared to case numbers.

The *Girmitiyas* took law often in hand for the dignity of women. Charles Andrews, an activist for Indian Independence and a close friend of Gandhi, has written:

"Indians can put up with poverty and torture. But they will never tolerate any kind of messing up with a woman's dignity."[28]

One *Kulambar* named Hall at Lautoka liked a *Girmitiya* woman named Piyari very much. One day while she was alone, he tried to force himself on her. She ran to the coolie lines and tried to kill herself but neighbours saved her in the nick of time. Subsequently three *Girmitiyas* Inderpal, Taan Singh and Gulab went to the bungalow of Hall and cut him to pieces. Police arrested seven innocent *Girmitiayas* on suspicion. The suspects were given death sentence by hanging and never pleaded their innonence, although they were. They died happily in the name of the dignity of women.[29]

Another incident concerns an Indian *Sardar*. Madre *Sardar* was enamoured by Som Naidu's wife Parvati. He tried to force himself on her one day in Som's absence. When Som came to know of this, he slit Madre's throat. Nobody suspected Som because he was crying his heart out in the *Shraddha* ceremony of Madre. After Madre's death, Som himself was appointed the *Sardar*. This time their *Kulambar* Brown set his heart on Parvati. He put Parvati's duty with him and sent a letter to Som to look for a new wife for himself. In a fit of rage Som chopped off Brown's leg, and carried him on his shoulders to Brown's bungalow looking for Parvati. Parvati had hanged herself on a noose made out of her saree. In a fit of anger Som chopped Brown to pieces there and then.[30]

A strange rule was that if a husband has completed his *Girmitiya* period and his wife was still serving, the husband was not allowed to enter Coolie Lines. Husbands would have to stay outside with children and wives would have to live there alone. In such a situation they faced more oppression. Many times, the *Sardars* sold off some *Girmitiya's* wife as well. The husband often killed himself when he came to know of it. On the other hand, there were some ambitious Indian women, who would enter relationship with European *Sardars* to get relaxations from work.

Expectant mothers were made to work till the last months of their pregnancy. Often the delivery (or abortion) would happen in the field itself. They did not even have experienced mid-wife to assist. As soon as they delivered, they had to get back to work. They didn't even have the permission to breastfeed their child during working hours. They would leave their crying babies in the Coolie Lines to come to work. One old *Girmitiya* midwife would take care of all these children. Their mothers would listen to them crying and try to guess whose child was crying. Many children would not survive for more than a few days. Children were buried there in the field and a stone was kept there to mark the grave.

The White men had learnt the word *randi* for whore. Often the supervisor *Kulambar* of women was teased as *randiwala.*[31] Once in the fields at Rarawai, the supervisor *Kulambar* of 30 women labourers came riding atop his horse and called a woman *randi* (whore). The women gathered and pulled him down from his horse, beat him up and then urinated on him. He felt so ashamed that he didn't dare to even complain and quietly returned to Australia. This shameful incident caused the company to prohibit people from troubling women.

Children lived in miserable conditions. In 1906 itself, 62% of *Girmitiya* children died on the island. There were no schools for them. They would keep playing in the ground near the Coolie Lines, most often *Gulli Danda*. Missionary schools were opened later, but it was not well received. Plantation owners believed that if the *Girmitiya* children received education, they could not be dominated easily. Worse still, if they became Christians, they would not obey them at all and would refuse to work in the fields.

Every Girmitiya child of 7 years and above who accompanied a *Girmitiya* on the ship automatically became a *Girmitiya* after he turned 12 and he was released only after five years of bonded labour.

(Fiji Indenture Ordinance,1891, Clause 58). This rule seems illegal at first instance because the child obviously had never signed on any agreement. Later this age was raised to 15 years but still this was without the consent of the child.

Even after getting free from the *Girmitiya* contract, people had huge debts and less income. Everybody wasn't exactly bankrupt though. If Shilling is measured against the Indian rupee, it had a stronger standing. But the expenses in Fiji were also thrice as much as in India. Labourers would eat less and live simply to save money. By the end of their period of bonded labour, some people would manage to save about 14 to 15 guineas. But these were also not enough for a livelihood after returning to India.

Hindustan in the hearts

Girmitiyas would often miss their homeland, especially their village. Often, they would write letters back home. In reply they would request them to come back. They were promised that they wouldn't be ostracised from the community, and they would be forgiven. To such letters the *Girmitiyas* wrote back that they were saving money to return. But that much money was probably never accumulated.

Budhai and Dhelai were about 25 when they left home along with their families saying that they were going for a *pooja* and would get some *prasad* from there. But they never returned. Someone saw them board a train to Calcutta, but nobody could testify it. Twenty years later, there came a letter from them alongwith ten pounds. Letter said that they are working in a sugar mill in Fiji and with this money they must get construct a well in the village. Their family members didn't even know where Fiji was. Even the most educated lawyer of the village was clueless. After a few years there was another letter stating that Dhelai had died in the mill. After many years there was another letter and some pictures. Usually, the *Girmitiyas* never returned.[32]

The elders in a *Girmitiya* household would narrate stories to children- of ghosts, witches, djinns, gods and goddesses. They had a treasure trove of tales which they brought from Hindustan. Each story had some moral lesson that was passed on to the current generation. Several stories were linked to the village. Like the grandfather of Fiji-born Rajendra Prasad would tell the tale of his village '*Belha Raghav*' Behraich (Uttar Pradesh.)

When in 1974 Rajendra Prasad was going on a visit to India, his *Girmitiya* grandmother said-

"Bachwa (son)! Go and make our front yard sacred again. If my brother or father is still around, seek forgiveness from them on my behalf. Tell them my heart is in turmoil. I shall die here only now."

He and his wife eventually reached their ancestral village, and they did find their estranged family as well, but this was a fortune reserved for only few. When he reached the village an elderly woman of the house said: -

"Ram and Sita have returned from exile."

Someone else asked, "One of my uncles went to *Chinidad,* did you meet him?"

"Trinidad is different, we are from Fiji."

To the villagers what was the difference between Trinidad and Fiji!

Gradually after India's independence, communication through letters became scant. They did know that a nephew had been born or a sister has been married. Most of them could never go back to the village. Regarding this Totaram writes in his book that when he wrote about his troubles in Fiji to his brother employed in Calcutta, he was so distressed that he passed away due to anguish three days later.[33] What kind of trouble can be so traumatic that barely the news of it can lead to death?

Girmitiyas would wear a dhoti and a white turban even in Fiji. Those who were *Ahirs* would raise a cow. They would also name the cow. Rajendra Prasad describes his cow *Hafkasiya* in his book as half-caste or hybrid. Cows were worshipped and never sold to the butcher. When it turned old it was left to roam in the forests of Kariya hill. Many *Ahirs* learnt horse-riding and could do cowboy-like stunts as well. Often there would be cirque among the labourers, this was a form of exercise particularly popular among Ahirs but anyone could participate. Sometimes there were wrestling matches among them too.

Fiji had a patriarchal society, (even today in several ways.) The father with his hefty moustache was the head of the family, and his children did not dare to speak to him directly. Children would tell their deepest thoughts to their mother, and she would convey it to the father. Women would cover their heads with an *odhni* (veil) in front of their father-in-law. Often, brothers along with their family would live in the same or adjacent houses.[34]

South Indian *Girmitiyas* were a minority and they could not converse properly with the North Indians. *Kulambars* also had learnt Hindi but could not speak Tamil. In utter loneliness some of them would kill themselves or would turn insane. Rajendra Prasad talks about a madman by the name of *Peddayya* who was Tamilian, but after five years as *Girmitiya* labour had forgotten his language. The villagers would ridicule him, and he would roam like a lunatic. He would hurl abuses in broken Hindi.

The relations with the natives of Fiji were limited. Many times, labourers would reach their villages after running away. They would in turn offer them food and shelter. They would also receive Indian food from them. Initially they didn't like *roti*, but later they started eating it and making it as well.

End of *Girmitiya* tradition

Gandhi's political guru Gopalkrishna Gokhale was aware of the atrocities on the *Girmitiyas* in Fiji since 1910 itself and he had written an application to the British. Mohandas Karamchand Gandhi had done a Satyagraha for the *Girmitiyas* of South Africa. This news reached Fiji too.

I have already discussed that Totaram Sanidhaya had written a letter to Gandhi.[35] After this, Gandhi sent a barrister named Manilal Maganlal, a lawyer, to Fiji in 1912. Manilal was a hardworking lawyer and had earlier fought a case in Mauritius. Because of him, in 1916 for the first time a *Girmitiya* named Badri Maharaj found a place in the legislative council. Although after joining the council Badri Maharaj remained a supporter of the British regime, but at least *Girmitiyas* got represented.

In 1915 Gandhi sent his friend Charles Andrews to Fiji to investigate the oppression of the *Girmitiyas*. He found a 15 years-old Brahmin teenager; whose hands were still soft, asking to be sent back to India. He had been lured to come here. Charles Andrews fought against British atrocities and has made a huge contribution to the abolition of bonded labour there. He was lovingly called *Deenbandhu* (Friend of poor people).

Girmitiyas attained freedom on 1 January 1920. Celebrations included burning effigies of CSR Company and the clothes of coolies. *Girmitiyas* hugged one another in joy. But this freedom wasn't permanent. They had to still work and wages were same. They decided to go on a strike which was led by Manilal's wife. On 13 February 1920, there was an encounter between the protestors and the police on the Sambabula bridge. The police opened fire and shot them ruthlessly. Many people died, although officially only one death was reported. It was a small bridge and there was a stampede. This was like the 'Jallianwala Bagh' of Fiji. On 15 April 1920 Manilal had to leave Fiji on charges of treason. Along with him, other protestors like Fazal Ahmed Khan and Harpal Maharaj were also declared traitors.[36]

Casteism and Religion in Fiji

Most of the *Girmitiyas* who were taken to Fiji was from the *Ahir, Kahaar, Kumhaar* and *Kurmi* communities. According to the figures available, the main caste-based divisions were as follows-

1. *Chamaar*-6087 (13%)
2. Muslim- 5455(12%)
3. *Ahir*-4197 (9%)
4. Thakur- 3416 (7.5%)
5. Other castes, Tribal people and South Indians[37]

Most of the people who came to Fiji were from Basti, Gonda and Faizabad districts (Appendix 5).

From South India they were brought from North Arcot, Madras, Krishna, Godavari, Vishakhapatnam, Tanjore and Coimbatore districts.

Labourers who were from Bihar were named after the day they were born. Those born on a Wednesday were named *Budh*, *BudhaI* (man), or *Budhia* (woman). For those on a Friday would be called *Shukra, Sukhai* and *Sukhiya*. Those born on a Saturday were named as *Shanichar* or *Shanichari*, and so on. Like all other *Girmitiya* countries, one good thing that happened in Fiji too was that the Hindu caste system vanished. Because women were lesser in number there were inter-caste marriages. There were marriages with the natives of Fiji too. Everybody was mostly in the same financial condition, so casteism lost its utility.

Caste segregation again kind of started in the middle of 20th century when they became freed and didn't remain a *Girmitiya* anymore. An *Ahir* would try to get his son married into an *Ahir* family or a higher caste but not to a *Chamar*. However, this practice didn't survive after 1950. Not everybody cares about the caste system in current day Fiji. Even if they know their caste, they might not be knowing about the others.

The children of *Girmitiyas* also read many religious books. Among them *Ramayana, Ram Charit Manas, Mahabharat, Sukh Sagar, Saling Sadabrij* and *Baital Pacchissi* were popular.[38] In moments of crisis, the *Hanuman Chalisa* was also read. Most labourers knew it by heart.

In 1902 the first *Ramlila* was organized in Novau. Labourers came on foot from far off places to witness it. Later, in 1909, Ramlila was organized in Ba. This tradition continued and got bigger. In *Ramlila* the natives would play the characters of the demon-army of Ravana. They portrayed the CSR Company as Ravana. Similarly, Muslims would take out *Taziya* procession in which Hindus also participated. South Indian people also performed worship in temples in which 'Tirnal' *nautanki* was popular. '*Bada Din*' or Christmas was equally popular, and people would eat mutton and drink that day. CSR Company held its own fairs, which was known as *Ullu Mela* (Owl Fair). The Whites would celebrate with the labourers and all would participate in games together.

Some Brahmins (as well as non-Brahmins) took preisthood as a profession and began flashing a '*Tripund*' mark on their forehead. They learnt the *Satyanaryan Katha* by heart, learnt to read the *Panchang* and perform some rituals. Not many of them were professionals. Five years of hard labour had made everybody's memories faint. Totaram Sanadhya was among the early preists of Fiji.

The ritual of *Shraddha* (death ceremony) also underwent changes. Hindu *Girmitiyas* were no longer cremated. They were buried in the field itself. Many *Girmitiya* still speak about seeing ghosts in the fields. Many *Girmitiya* would turn insane, roaming around in jute clothes. People would say that they are possessed by ghost. After attaining freedom, North Indian *Girmitiyas* began to cremate their dead again and South Indians began to bury them. In the initial days, the *Kabirpanthi* people would carry out the task of burying the dead.[39] The *Shraddha* ritual would consist of Thirteen days of *Bhagavat Katha* recital, followed by a series of *Bhajan* recitals, and then wailing. In such times, the song, *Kaun Thagwa Nagariya Lootal Ho* (Some cheat has looted my city) was popular.

Missionaries tried to influence and convert these people. They were kind to these labourers. Especially priest Burton and his wife did several things for the welfare of the labourers. Besides them, a missionary woman named Miss Dudly, was called 'mother' by the *Girmitiyas*. But conversions were almost equal to none at that time. On one hand, the labourers did not trust Christianity as a religion and on the other the managers didn't want anybody to convert.

Fiji Hindi

Fiji Hindi is a strange admixture of several regional languages of India. A separate grammar was formed, and many foreign words also got included in their distorted forms. It was called Hindustani language. Gradually this has evolved a lot and now it is the mother tongue of most residents of Fiji.

In the last ships from Madras, about 15000 Tamil, Telugu and Malayalam speaking people arrived, but by then Hindi was well-established in Fiji. But they enriched Fiji Hindi by adding many Tamil and Telugu words. Later Punjabi and Gujarati speaking people also joined. Their families might speak Punjabi or Gujarati in their homes but they are fluent in Fiji Hindi. Many Fiji natives or Europeans who live in the Indian-majority areas of Fiji also speak and understand Fiji Hindi well.

Fiji Hindi is like Khari Boli in India but does have distortions: it has the flavour of *Poorvanchal* (Eastern part of North India). Like 'sha' is written and spoken as 'sa', 'va' as 'ba'. *Videsh* is called *Bides* in Fiji Hindi. Besides, the words with a lower accent (*nukta*) are also missing. Instead of *Phal* it is *Fal*, instead of *Zameen* it is *Jameen*. Words are more from the Avadhi and Bhojpuri languages. *Bhabhiji* (sister-in-law) is *Bhouji*. *Gaay* (Cow) is called *Gaiyya*. *Karm* became *Karam*, *Dharm* became *Dharam*, Rajendra became *Rajen*.

The verb is also used differently. *Hum aata hai.* (Present). *Ham kaal aayis.* (Past) *Hum bihaan aayega.* (Future). *Hum jaat raha. Hum dher khela karta tha. U aaiys. O aaiyn.*[40]

There are no plurals as well in Fiji Hindi. *Ek ghar, dui ghar, dher ghar. Ee log, dui log, dher log.* Although sometimes plurals are used in a different way. *Ek larka* (one boy), *dher larkan* (many boys.) *Ek admi, dher admiyan.* There is one more use. Like *ek larakwa* (one specific boy). *Larka* means any boy.

Saying '*ee*' instead of *ye, ee log, oo log, o log, wahi loga.*[41]

Some words were native of Fiji, especially for things that are found in Fiji only. For instance, the name of a sea fish. They call mullet fish, *kanade. Saala*, wife's husband is known as *tabaley*. Nangona is a *kahwa*-like drink which is had in the cups made of coconut shells known as *bilo*. There are words of English origin too, like *hutal* from hotel, *garaund* from ground, *geng* meaning gang, *ticha* meaning woman teacher.

Many words are different from how they are used in India. In Fiji an acre is a *beegha*. Tomorrow is known as *bihaan*. Bankrupt/*kangaal* is *fokatiya*. Lie is called *gupp*. Excessively beautiful is known as '*julum*.

What/*kya* is *konchi*. Door is known as *palla*. Everything is alright/*sab theek hai* is *sab set haii*.

Numerals also have a slight difference. Maybe the people from this community counted like this in India as well. Like forty-two/*byalis* is *chaalis aur dui*. Thirty-six/*chhatees* is *tees aur cheh*. The words *lakh*/ million and *krod*/billion do not exist in Fiji. Hundred thousand/*sau hazar* is used instead.

The script of Fiji Hindi is both Devnagari and English. The Bible has been translated into Fiji Hindi and it is now being taught as a language at the University of South Pacific. Raymond Pillai is an Indian Fijian. A film has been made based on his play *Adhoore Sapne*. A writer named Subramani wrote a novel named *Duaka Puraan* (maybe a derivative of *Dwarka Purana*) which is a satire written in the *Purana* format. Urmila Prasad has written a book in Roman script about Fiji Hindi, *Susamachar aur Romeo*.

Marriages in Fiji

In the *Girmitiya* times, only court marriages happened, without any music or pomp. The fee was 50 cents. There was no system of dowry. In later years, a *pandit* would find an auspicious date and match the horoscopes of the bride and groom.

The rituals of marriage were very long. On the first day was '*telvaan*' in which oil and turmeric would be applied on the groom and bride's body. A *Mandap*/altar would be set up. Women would sing and dance. On the second day '*bhatvan*' other formalities were done and next day was the *Shaadi*. 50-100 people would go in the *Baraat*. Initially, only men used to go, but later women also started accompanying them. *Hijra* dance and Qawwali was also popular in many villages. After spending one night at the bride's place, the next day the groom would take the bride to his house. Drums, *manjira* and timpano were played at that time. People would dance. But these rituals could be performed by a free *Girmitiya* only. When the bride was taken in a *doli* to her husband's house, this song was popular-

"Shivji byahne chale paalki sajayi ke bibhuti lagaye ka o na"

Lord Shiva is going to get married on a carriage, and adorning a head mark

At the arrival of the *doli,* this song was played-

"Le ke doliya kahaar baaje, baaje, baaje shehnayi hamaare angna"

The carriage driver is going, while the trumpet is being played.

Those people who would do the work of matchmaking were known as *Nabu.* Their wives, known as *Nabuniya*, would also participate with vigour in this. They would travel from one village to another with a proper list and details of brides and grooms and bring proposals. The moment a *Nabu* would come riding on a horse to the village, people would guess that someone was getting married. Everybody would surround the *Nabu*, who was usually a chatterbox. He would bring tons of news--this one got married here, that boy is good, that one has so much land. But in successive generations *Nabus* lost their utility. There were many *bhagau* or runaway marriages too. However, marriage was an event in which the entire village offered support and help.

I was watching a Fiji marriage video-

The groom arrived in car bedecked with flowers. Outside the bride's house, people were playing drums, timpano and hand cymbals. There was a *pipihi*-player too (an instrument like a *shehnai*). The song being played was was the popular Hindi song, '*Raja ki aayegi baarat*.' This went on for a while. All the time, the groom remained seated in his car. The groom was of Tamil origin and bride of Bihar origin. But both the families spoke in Hindustani (Fiji Hindi).

After a while, many women came out of the bride's place wearing Kanjeevaram silk sarees. They came and opened the door of the groom's car. Wearing a silk kurta, the groom appeared to be somewhat shy. As he stepped out, the women performed some ritual using rice. Then they extended a canopy of a silk sheet over the groom's head under which he walked ahead. The saree-clad women finally brought the groom to the courtyard of the house. There the Pandit read some *shlokas* (sacred chants) in Sanskrit and made him sit in the *mandap* (marriage court). The *pipihi*-player played- '*badi dur se aaye hain pyar ka taufa laaye hain*' (We have come from far away, brought the gift of love).

After that several women surrounded the groom, one was putting a mark (*tilak*) on his forehead and another was doing aarti. This went on for quite some time. In the background several Hindi songs are playing-- some new, some old and some folk. All the while, a *pandit ji was* delivering a lecture of some sort in chaste Hindi in front of the men sitting in the veranda. He was saying-

"Today on this great occasion the confluence of two families is taking place, two villages, North and South. It is our great fortune that we can participate in this good event. Let's hope the relationships between these two families remain pleasant."

Sanskrit *mantras* were being chanted and a coconut was placed on the fire burning in the middle and the marriage was solemnised. Then he announced that from this day this daughter now belongs to your house. Members of both families began to dance. The *Pipihi*-player played many songs. Everybody was dancing in a rustic manner. A woman then began to sing a Bhojpuri song, reading out the lyrics from a thin booklet. But the sound of the hand-cymbals, harmonium and *pipihi* drowned her voice.

At last, the groom and the bride stood up and people got pictures clicked. It was followed by a feast. All the people from the *baraat* and from the bride's side partook the food. It seemed as if the marriage was taking place in some village in India.

Post-*Girmitiya* Fiji

When the *Girmitiya* tradition ended and everybody was free, they wanted to forget their odious past. They didn't sing the '*bidesiya*' of those days. They wouldn't tell the children what they had endured. There were some permanent scars on their bodies about which they would make some excuses. They did not want to write their history. History is created by the victorious not the defeated. The British wanted to hide it and the Indians wanted to bury it. In the schoolbooks of Fiji there isn't much about *Girmitiyas*. In 1921 Banarsidas Chaturvedi wrote a book called *Fiji ki Samasya* (The Problems of Fiji) which was later burnt in Fiji. By the 70s all *Girmitiyas* had died and with them their past was buried too. The British Government also never appreciated them. Their sacrifice and their hard work, all have been overlooked.

It is pertinent to me to solve this puzzle that how the *Girmitiya* people who were brought here in a slavery-like tradition from far off land became the rulers of this country. How did they become prime Minister and controlled the economy of the country? Is this actually the golden period or just an illusion? Would this migrant community be forced to migrate again?

In 1930, the *Girmitiya* tradition ended but CSR Company still ruled. The freed labourers took land on lease from the company, but the laws were still not obsolete. *Kulambars* still held influence. The moment his horse would enter the village people would call out to each other and disappear into their houses. Whoever came across him would have to greet him. If he responded to their greeting, they would feel grateful as of some god had heard their prayers. In 1939, *Kulambar* Evan was annoyed with labourer Perimal. He first threw Perimal's belongings out and then burnt his hut. The entire night Perimal and his family sat under a mango tree across the road.[42] Similarly, Nageshwar Prasad had to vacate his land because he did not greet a *Kulambar*.

At last, a *Girmitiya* named Ayodhya Prasad formed a *Kisaan Sangh* and went from village to village fighting for the rights of farmers. This association became so strong that a rule had to be made that no *Kulambar* could abuse any farmer. From the background of *Pandit* Totaram and *Pandit* Ayodhya, one can deduce that they could come up with such plans because they were educated. Hence the Whites were right in their apprehension that by taking *Girmitiyas* from higher castes they were risking their own future. Other than the *Kisaan Sangh*, famous lawyer Ahmedbhai Patel established the *Mahasangh* in 1941. Both the organizations had several members.

Girmitiyas began to participate in the politics of the country. Badri Prasad was already in the Council, later in 1929 *Pandit* Vishnu Dev, Parmanand Singh and James Ramchandra were also elected. But one leader who stood out and worked for everyone's welfare was Shivabhai Bhailalbhai Patel. He was sent in 1927 by Gandhiji to help the residents of Fiji. He started this work and continued till the end of the 70s.

Many other equations were also changing after the freedom of the *Girmitiyas*. The natives of Fiji and the *Girmitiyas,* both were campaigning against the Whites in different ways. The Whites fuelled the conflict between these two groups which is still the main cause of conflict in Fiji.

In 1934 Governor Fletcher recruited people of Indian origin and Indian labourers into their army and formed an Indian platoon. They tried to combine the Indian people with them so that they could stand by them in their conflict with the tribal people of Fiji. European army men would get 4 shillings per day whereas Fiji natives and Indians would get only 2 shillings. Indian men revolted against their lesser wages. Finally, in 1950 the Indian platoon had to be abolished.

After attaining freedom, internal conflicts among the Indians also arose. *Pandits* and *Maulvis* began their respective religious propaganda. On one hand, Hindu-Muslim discord was rising and on the other, among the Hindus also many caste-based groups were formed. *Sanatan Dharma, Arya Samaj, Kabir Panth, Satnami, Nanak, Ramanadi*, various such groups came into existence. Especially the dispute between *Sanatan Dharamis* and *Arya Samajis* continued for many years. In 1926 the Fiji Muslim League was established. In the the same year South Indians formed the *Sangam* group and *Punjabis* the *Gurudwara Samiti.*

But one good thing happened, all these organizations opened several schools. Till 1938 there were 7968 students in 71 schools. In Hindu schools, the medium of instruction was Hindi, in Muslim schools it was Urdu, and in Tamil schools it was Tamil. But later most schools became English medium. Fiji Indians began to realize that their terrible condition was due to the lack of education. In those days the schools that were good were DAV College, Rarawai Muslim School, Wakiya (Methodist) Indian school, Waysuru Indian School and Khalsa College. It wasn't so easy to open schools, but all farmers gave away some land and invested some money for it. The government did not give any funds to these schools, and they ran on the capital of these independent *Girmitiyas*. It is because of these schools only that Fiji Indians have made huge progress, and most of them turned into skilled professionals. Some Indians still manage family-owned farms.

Indian children were more disciplined compared to Fiji native children. This also proves that being from a *Dalit* or *Brahmin* background or being from the labour class did in no way affect anyone's learning potential. They all lived in penury, devoid of luxuries and comforts. Their children were also hardworking like their parents and walked 10-12 km through mountains and forests to reach school and after returning helped their father in the fields as well. Many didn't even own a pair of shoes.

After the end of the *Girmitiya* tradition, the government give the farmers the earnings from their sugarcane crop twice a year, and all kids of the family would wait for these two days. They would go to the fair, buy things and play, while the adults drank alcohol. Because big earning would happen only on these two days annually, for the rest of the year they would borrow money from the village moneylender at the rate of 40% interest. Whatever money they received, that too they kept with shopkeepers or moneylenders and got some interest out of it. But there was no written guarantee of this money. Once, one shopkeeper Pillai went bankrupt, so many who had kept their money with him, lost their money too.[43]

Among the bonded labour, a few were fortunate enough to get land on lease from Europeans where they would on work weekends or evenings. Some also owned cows and sold vegetables in the market.

Till the 70s, Fiji Indians lived in mud huts known as *bures*, but gradually they began to make paved houses with weathered-tiled roofs. White *Kulambars* had their grand houses atop the hills. Homes would have cots and lofts were also made in trees. Often kitchens were kept away from the main house for fire safety. Food was cooked on mud stoves and women used narrow pipes to blow and flame the fire. There were no taps in the house so people would dig wells or get water from the river. People would use the *datuan* (green twigs) to clean their teeth. However, by the 60s, toothpastes and powders had made an appearance.

Each home would also have a small temple, where the women would light a lamp after cleaning it. Villages had plenty of rumourmongers. Any news would spread in the village like wildfire. Villages would have some small shops where people would gather and indulge in chitchat. Often people would have credit accounts there. Domestic disputes and beating of wives were also commonplace in the villages.

A regional newspaper *Shantidoot* was quite popular. An educated villager would read out aloud from it to others, especially people would rejoice in listening to news about India. In the 50s they also got the radio, but it needed a bamboo antenna on the roof. Religious programmes on radio had a wide audience. Especially those which talked of various rituals and obituaries. Later there were football commentary too and it made radio more popular.

Gulli danda is now extinct but football is popular. There was no game more inexpensive than this for *Girmitiya* children. There was no dearth of grounds. Later, all islands had their own teams who played matches among themselves. Professional football began with Lloyd Fairbrother Trophy which was held every year.

There was a local player named Rai Krishna. Chandrabhan Singh was a famous mid-fielder. People say nobody in Fiji was better than him. Johnny Bakridi was a fighter. People would provoke him and then he would kick someone and would be expelled, but he was a good player. A mid-fielder named Chhotka later went to Sydney and became a taxi driver there. Many years before that Anand Sami was also famous, although later, he also went to Brisbane. He and his brother Jagannath Sami were known as Soccer Princes. Jagannath Sami later became a famous politician in Fiji and the CEO of the Sugarcane Traders Association. Though later after a military coup he was thrown out of power. On football fields, Whites, Indians and natives all played together. This was one field where all discrimination ceased.

Football also had some special words. Like '*Aawe, Awwe*' meant 'he is coming'. Similarly, '*Le lo, le lo*.' When the chances of goals were few, they would say '*Ee na jaayi*.' If the referee gave a wrong decision, he was called a '*murgi-chor*'.[44]

Only Whites were allowed in clubs, halls and golf-courses. 'No Indians Allowed' was written there. Trains had 'Whites only' compartments. Even when council members like Muniswamy Mudliyar went to meet the *Sahebs* he was told to sit on the floor.

On 10 October 1970, Fiji became an independent country. But with this independence came an overwhelming nationalism. In 1969 the biggest leader of Fiji Indians, A. D. Patel passed away. Fiji Indians again seemed to be at the brink of being homeless. In 1972 when Idi Amin threw 80,000 Indian people out of Uganda, Indians on Fiji also got scared. In 1975 the leader of Fiji Nationalist Party Sakeasi Butadroka proposed in the parliament:

"It is time now that all Indians and people of Indian origin return to their own country, and the expenses for sending them to be borne by the British government who brought them here."

Although this proposal wasn't passed but it led to a fear among Fiji Indians. But amidst all this, the 100th year of Fiji *Girmitiya* was celebrated well in 1979. In 1981 Indian primeminister Indira Gandhi made a trip to Fiji and in subsequent years many people from the successive governments visited there.

Then, something happened which pushed Fiji Indians to the corner. On 24 March 1987, a procession was taken out saying, 'Stop this government of the Indians, this is Fiji and not mini-India.' This was the Taukei Movement, the rebel of the Fiji natives. These people attacked Indians and did bomb blasts at many places. On 14 May 1987, Colonel Rabuka stormed into parliament and captured all the leaders.

Atrocities began on Fiji Indians, but they didn't rebel against it. How would *Girmitiya* blood rebel? Indian leaders Vinod Patel and Dwijendra Singh were dragged by their hair and put in prison. Temples, mosques, gurudwaras were all burnt. This continued for at least a decade and then suddenly in 1997 Colonel Rabuka softened his stance. The economy of the country was gradually weakening, and he realized that the country can't run properly without the Indians.

In 1999 there were elections and Mahendra Pal Chaudhary was elected Prime Minister, the first PM of Indian origin. At last, *Girmitiya* reached the throne, and this day is a glorious day in the history of Fiji. But the victory was transient.

Next year itself a group of rebels under the leadership of George Spite reached parliament and held Mahendra Chaudhary and all other leaders, captive. They were held hostage in the parliament for 56 days and atrocities on Indians continued outside. Fiji natives began to loot and kill Indians. Many people say that had the Whites brought Sikhs and *Kshatriya* people as *Girmitiya,* the scenario would have been quite different. Dalit and lower caste people didn't have the fire to rebel in them. They were used to oppression from feudal India itself. George Spite was later captured and sent to jail. But many Fiji Indians migrated during this crisis to Australia, New Zealand, America, Canada and England. Wherever they went they worked hard and are now among the richest families there.

Fault lies with Indian *Girmitiyas* too. Like the *Girmitiyas* of other countries they did not mingle with the natives. They made their own group, their own party, kept speaking their own language and were unable to forge a contact with the Fiji culture. They ended up being a mini-India. They didn't become Christians and chose to stay as Hindus. They focused on education and hard work, whereas natives were neither hardworking nor educated. These gap kept on widening.

Forty percent of Fiji population are Indians. About 4,50,000 people of Indian origin are currently (2017) in Fiji. Those who migrated during the 1987 coup to Australia and New Zealand are about sixty thousand and speak Fiji Hindi. They have kept their Fijian culture alive, and they consider themselves distinct from other Indians living in Australia. Besides this, there are more than 30,000 Fiji Indians in America and Canada as well.

As per my analysis, in these two islands of Mauritius and Fiji, Indians have maintained their Indianness the most. Whether it was good or bad for them is a separate issue.

References

1. Rajendra Prasad, *Tears in Paradise: Suffering and Struggles of Indians in Fiji 1879-2004*, Glade Publishers, 2004 (Secondary Source)
2. Swati Mathur, How this Fiji Girmitiya found his India home, Times News Network, 7th January 2016
3. Totaram Sanidhaya and Banarsi Das Chaturvedi, <u>*Fiji* Dweep mein mere Eekees Varsh,</u> Rajput Anglo Oriental Press, 1914

4. Peter Dillon, Narrative and successful result of a voyage in the South Seas, Hurst Chance &Company. 1829 (Courtesy Yale University Library)
5. Ibid.
6. I C Campbell, The Historiography of Charles Savage, *Journal of Polynesian Society*, 1980, 89(2), page 143-166
7. J W Davidson, Peter Dillon of Vanikoro: Chevalier of the South Seas, Oxford University Press, Melbourne, 1975, p. 31
8. www.girmit.org (Internet source)
9. Basil Lubbock, *Coolie Ships and Oil Sailers*, Brown, Son & Ferguson, 1981
10. BBC documentary, Coolies: How Britain Reinvented Slavery
11. Rajendra Prasad , op. cit., Secondary source
12. Totaram, op cit.
13. Rajendra Prasad, op. cit.
14. Totaram, op.cit.
15. Rajendra Prasad op. cit.
16. Ibid.
17. Pandit Gurdayal Sharma, *Memories of Fiji, 1887-1987*, Self-published, Suva, 1987
18. Totaram, op.cit.
19. Walter Gill, Turn Northeast at Tombstone, Robert Hail Limited, 1970
20. Totaram , op. cit.
21. Rajendra Prasad ref.1 Secondary source
22. Same as ref.1
23. John Burton, Fiji of Today, Charles H Kelly, 1910
24. Rajendra Prasad ref.1 Secondary source
25. Same as ref.1
26. Same as ref.1
27. Same as ref.1
28. Same as ref.1
29. Gurdayal ref.17
30. Rajendra Prasad ref.1 Secondary source
31. Same as ref.1
32. Same as ref.1
33. Totaram ref.3
34. Rajendra Prasad ref.1 Secondary source
35. Same as ref.1
36. Same as ref.1
37. Brij Lal, Girmitiyas the origin of Fiji Indians, Journal of Pacific History 1983
38. Rajendra Prasad ref.1
39. Same as ref.1
40. Rodney Mog an Ram Narayan, Fiji Hindi: A basic course and Reference Grammar, Courtesy Australian Univeristy press extension services, University of South Pacific, Suva (Fiji), 1977
41. Same ref.40
42. Rajendra Prasad ref.1 Secondary source
43. Same ref.1
44 Brij Lal, Intersections: History, Memory and Discipline, NSUE press, 2012
45. Fiji population up 50,0000 in 10 years, Fiji LIVE, 31st October 2017

Guyana

"Every foreign land is fatherland, and every fatherland is foreign land."
- Letter to Diognetus

Illusory Lacchman

Lacchman was taken to Guyana deceitfully by an *Arkati* agent. He was told that in Guyana, he would just have to lie down, coconut water would fall into his mouth and there will be gold everywhere. When he reached there, things were much different. His dream world was shattered. He was instead sent to toil in the fields.

Lacchman ran away from the plantation, in fact, the second time. It wasn't easy to run away from the plantation. If one was caught, it meant imprisonment. But Lacchman would often go missing for a few days and then again return. Nobody knew his whereabouts. He kept running away and returning back. He would tell his friends that one day he would make his way back to India. Everybody tried to convince him that it was impossible, and he must accept his fate. Lacchman spent ten years on the island and in 1884, he was lost. Neither he nor his dead body was found anywhere on the island. His passport had been withheld by the plantation owner but surprisingly it was heard that he did manage to reach India!

What is even more unbelievable is that the very next year Lacchman returned to Guyana on the ship *Allenshaw* only to run away again after three months. This time the plantation owner received a letter from London. Lacchman had somehow reached England. In 1887, Lacchman again returned to Guyana with a forged identity and said that he had come from Natal (Africa). But the officials recognized him. He ran away again but was caught on his way to Suriname.

In 1888 Lacchman ran away for the last time, and nobody heard of him ever again. The illusory Lacchman of Guyana remained a mystery man.[1] I shall discuss again about Lacchman in a crucial context later.

Love Story of a White Man

A beautiful upper caste woman Janaki was lured by *Arkati* from some village in United province. In villages such beautiful women were often married off early to a boy from an affluent family. But many women felt trapped and wanted to fly away and see the world. Nobody knows when Janaki fell into the trap of an *Arkati*. The agent must have received a handsome amount for bringing such a beautiful woman.

Janaki was brought to the Demerara depot of Garden Reach in Calcutta. Tired of the long journey, she bathed and changed into provided new clothes. She was dreaming of Guyana island, a heaven as told by *Arkati,* where she would live like a princess.

In 1882, the ship *Silhouette* set sail for Guyana. The *Sardars* on the ship already had their eyes on her, especially one named Dee Mohammad. He was a Muslim but was totally smitten by Janaki. He would look after Janaki and she in turn paid some attention to the well-built man. Being a *Sardar*, he was well-respected, so it seemed her dream of becoming a princess was about to come true.

But Janaki had another suitor on the ship—the English surgeon Dr. Atkins. His father, Reverend Atkins, was a supporter of slavery abolition. Most likely Atkins also supported it. Otherwise, it wasn't common for an Englishman to fall in love with a *Girmitiya* woman. There would be many who would sexually exploit them, but few would fall in love with them.

Though Dee Mohammad was a *Sardar* but in front of a White officer, he fell short. He had to abandon all hopes of Janaki, as she too preferred Dr. Atkins over him. After reaching Guyana, Atkins sent an application to get Janaki's contract cancelled and requested that she should be set free. He had to pay 250 pounds for her release.

His letter was sent to London and Janaki was freed. They got married in Georgetown. This unusual marriage of 19th century is still recorded in books.[2]

But what isn't recorded is what happened to Janaki after marriage. Dr. Atkins first went to Australia, then England and then returned to India. He died in Calcutta on 3rd July 1896, fourteen years after his marriage with Janaki. But Janaki cannot be traced. There is no mention whether Dr. Atkins took her along or left her back in Guyana itself. Can you guess what might have happened to Janaki? Abandoned, died or lived like a queen?[3]

Maharani an incomplete journey

When the ship *Allenshaw* set sail for Guyana, there were many unusual incidents happening on board. Illusory Lacchman was going back to Guyana in that ship. But this story is about a woman named Maharani. A research student Verne Shepherd investigated Maharani's mysterious death on board.

Maharani was an eighteen-year-old upper caste girl. Her father's name was Pargas. It is quite possible that such a young girl was abducted by an *Arkati* or else duped into eloping with him. She mostly remained quiet on the ship. One morning Dr. Hardvick found Maharani covered in a blanket on an upper deck.

She was running high fever. Dr Hardvick sent her to the lower deck with some medicines. He didn't ask what had happened to Maharani. She kept crying the entire night, so her companions Nandlal and Golop took her again to the doctor. Dr. Hardvick now suspected that something strange must have happened, but he could not fathom what it was. Maharani kept complaining of body ache, which was quite common on the ship. Next morning her heartbeat began to faint and she passed away. How did she die?

Researcher Shepherd found some papers of two women witnesses named Murti and Mahodaya whom Maharani had told that she had been raped. Not by just one man but at least three men. When one night Maharani went to the upper deck to fill water, two sailors held her and covered her mouth and raped her one after the other. Initially the witnesses claimed that one of them was a black man, Robert Ipsen. The second was James Oliver from England, and the third an unknown person.

Mahodaya knew Maharani back from India. Maharani told her before dying that one of the men had a tattoo mark on his chest. Same man had abused one Jogesar's wife earlier as well. This man could be Robert Ipsen because he had in fact abused Jogesar's wife earlier. Two other Indians also suspected Robert Ipsen as he had told them back in Calcutta itself that he intended to do something of this sort on the ship. An officer named Thomas David said that Robert Ipsen had confessed sexual assault in front of him, but he didn't mention the name of the woman. Ipsen had even shown him a penis wound caused due to the incident. One more witness Li also said that he had often seen Ipsen put his hand around Maharani's shoulder, though he had warned Ipsen to avoid such acts. But Li admitted that he hadn't seen any one sexually assaulting her.

But why didn't Maharani complain about this incident? Maybe she was scared. When after Murti and Mahodaya's complaint, the officer on the ship had again asked Maharani in the hospital, she denied and said that nothing of the sort had happened. Probably she didn't trust the Whites. After interrogation of the suspects, as soon as Robert Ipsen alighted from the ship, he was arrested. Although as per the post-mortem report by Dr. Hardvik there was no evidence of rape. His opinion was that if rape had happened a few days ago, it was difficult to ascertain. Dr. Hardvik could only certify that Maharani had died due to shock, but the reason was unknown.

After alighting from the ship Mahodaya changed her statement and said that Maharani was friendly with these sailors beforehand. She alleged that usually they would go in groups of twos and threes to fill water but that day, Maharani deliberately went alone. She said that she had confided to her about having sex but didn't say that it was forced. Possibly Mahodaya changed her statement because she was threatened. The second witness Murti also retracted her earlier statement.

However, it was clearly evident from the witness account that the cause for her stomach pain had been forceful sex.

At this point Lacchman enters the story. He presented an entirely different story. He had relationships with many women including those on board this ship. One major witness in this case, Murti, was Lacchman's companion or lover on the ship. There were rumours that Lacchman was involved with Maharani too. Apparently, Lacchman's friend Chitaman was an eyewitness to this rape which lasted about 45 minutes. When Maharani was admitted to the hospital, he even went to enquire about her health. Chitaman also told that two White men and one black man were involved.

Statement of the accused Robert Ipsen was pointing towards another direction. He said that sailors and officers often had sexual relations on the ship. *Girmitiya Sardars* often helped in this. For a meagre bribe like some extra tobacco, they would bring the women to the sailor's or officer's room. He blamed the senior officers of the ship for this crime. He said that often officers gave better food to the women they liked or favoured. He had seen doctors and officers make women sit on chairs and put their hands between their legs. He knew Maharani through Lacchman. Since she was either his or his friends' lover, hence he had never cast eyes on her in that way. According to Ipsen, Lacchman had told him that the White officers wanted to frame him.

In the end, the incident remains a mystery. Maharani could have died after contracting some sexually transmitted disease or shock after forced sex. All the accused were finally acquitted. The case files of Maharani lies buried somewhere in Guyana.[4]

A soldier's trip to Demerara, 1870

Girmitiya didn't always mean some poor agrarian from rural India. Some English-speaking young men too had taken those ships.

One afternoon, Mohammad Sharif was shopping some flowers in a busy Lucknow market when he happened to meet an *Arkati.*

"Are you looking for work? You can come with me to Demerara. The sugarcane plantations there give plenty of money".

"Is that so? I would surely like to come".

Sharif had recently found a job in the infantry division of the army, but he quitted it. He didn't want to let go off this opportunity. Along with Sharif, nine more people were sent to Calcutta on a train and on 25th August they left for Guyana on board a ship called *Mediya*. There were 446 Indians along with Sharif on that ship, with 91 women, 31 children and 21 infants among them. The ship took 87 days to reach there. During this journey 6 people died and 5 children were born.

Sharif was intelligent, educated and could speak fine English. He was soon chosen as *Sardar* on the ship, and he also acted as an interpreter for the Whites. He was supposed to get three dollars for this work but never got paid fully. The *Arkati* agent had also promised him a bonus, which of course he never got either.

Two years ago, he had been to Ethiopia to help as a member of British forces. Ship journey wasn't a new experience for him. That is why he was more confident than the other seafarers on that ship. Sharif had never done farming in his life but had served in the army, so he was fit and well-built. He spent ten years in Guyana. But I could not get the information how was his stay in Guyana? Did he ever return to India?[5]

Pregnant, 4 months

Village-Burahupur, Police District Majhi, District- Chhapra

A four-months pregnant Brahmin woman Sujariya was being taken to Faizabad depot by an *Arkati* and then she was moved to Calcutta. She reached Guyana on the ship *Clyde*. There is no record about her husband. She gave birth to a boy on this ship and named him Lal Bahadur. Many years later, in 2005, her great granddaughter Gaiutra Bahadur came to Bihar in search of her ancestors. She traced this inspiring and mysterious journey in her book *Coolie Woman*. Many agonizing tales are referenced here from her book.

She could only find this much in the records that Sujariya's father was called Mukhlal. Maybe someone in the village would remember about him. In those days if a Brahmin woman ran away from her home, it surely was a scandalous event. That too a pregnant woman from an affluent family.

Burahupur is a small village of about 8000 Bhojpuri speaking farmers. Gaiutra finally found a person whose great grandfather Mukhlal Dubey died in the Burma war. Mukhlal Dubey had one daughter named Ramjaro or Shivjaro? Gaiutra assumed that the English must have noted her name as *Sujariya*.

Whoever she was, at the age of mere twenty-seven she set for a long voyage and gave birth to a child during journey, whose descendants now live in America. While her ancestral village is still backward, this woman from Chhapra had stepped out to make history.

In Guyana, Sujariya began to live with a *Girmitiya* Thakur Shivratan Singh and his wife. She had a daughter later with Shivratan Singh. Due to some reason, Sujariya left her son Lal Bahadur with him and took her daughter away. Its difficult to conclude what kind of relationship they both shared.

On another plantation far away, she was in a relation with an *Ahir* man named Dilchand with whom she had another daughter. Even after estrangement, her relations with Shivratan's family were cordial. They would often come to meet her. Fourteen years after the death of Shivratan Singh, her firstborn son on the ship, Lal Bahadur, got re-connected with her.

The name 'Bahadur' was carried forward by the successors of this courageous woman. It bears special significance that this wasn't a patriarchal last name. This was a last name granted by a mother to her son.

Sujariya's life is a talc of the struggles and the various stages of an indentured seafaring woman.[6]

The Maine, 1901

It rarely happened that a *Girmitiya* ship halted midway unless there was a technical issue or a revolt aboard the ship.

One black sailor Sted misbehaved with some woman outside the poop. The secluded area near the poop was notorious for such incidents of molestation. Due to this, women would often go there in groups. If someone was caught alone, sailors would block her way and sexually harass her. Many times, they would try to lure these women with some biscuits or cashews. Surgeon General Dr. Oliver had seen Sted harassing a woman and he was quite upset about it.

All the sailors were summoned, and they were reminded about the rules and regulations, but the blacks were in greater number, and they all stood by Sted. The sailors revolted against Dr. Oliver and the issue took a serious turn. Dr. Oliver had to finally take out his gun and the ship was forcibly halted midway in Mauritius. There Sted and one of his companions were arrested and jailed and then only the ship proceeded. Dr. Oliver's bold and unprecedented step for women's dignity must be remembered.[7]

Ship was in such a poor condition that all the voyagers became weak during the journey. Due to this revolt, they did not get food properly. One woman admitted that she had sold her body to an officer for some food. Since plantation owners would not pay for weak labourers, they were fed adequately for a few days at Georgetown. But their condition was so bad that two hundred people had to be admitted to the hospital. The rest of the labourers were sent to the plantations, but they fell sick within a few days. While the revolt saved dignity of women, the consequences had to borne by the *Girmitiyas*.

Seafarers' revolt aboard *Ezel*, 1875

St. Helena island was one common stopover but a strange incident happened that day. As soon as the 'protector of agreement' came for a surprise inspection on the ship, a group of *Girmitiya* women fell on his feet. They were crying and shouting something in their language, which inspector didn't comprehend. They used sign language to convey that they were being subjected to ill treatment by the ship's doctor Holleman. They insisted that if the doctor wasn't taken off the ship, they would kill themselves or slit the throat of this doctor. This was an unprecedented incident because usually the women seafarers remained quiet. This was a rare example of an organised revolt on a ship.

One woman complained that the surgeon had forcibly raped her for three nights continuously. Another woman reported that he had dragged her forcibly into his room and raped her. She had complained later but nobody paid any heed. One woman reported that her mouth had been gagged and then raped. Another woman said that the surgeon often groped her and molested her on several occasions. One woman named Ramjhadi said she was given some biscuits and asked to go to his cabin at night. When she refused, she was kept handcuffed for ten hours.

Dr. Holleman was deboarded. In spite of serious sexual harassment charges, no further action was taken against him. As a physician also, Dr. Holleman's record was bad. 31% people had died on the ship under his supervision, which was the highest death rate in *Girmitiya* history. Still, he was retained for many years as a doctor on ship. It is quite possible that he kept on sexually harassing women for many years to come.[8]

Theft of an unborn child from the Womb

Eliza James was a black woman who fell in love with an Indian man named Sukool. Sukool was the manager of the child labourers of the plantation. Although, love relationships between blacks and Indians were not common, in fact they were always at loggerheads. Eliza and Sukool soon started living together. Eliza loved him very much and even learnt his native language.

Since Eliza could not bear him a child, Sukool remained upset. Eliza hatched a plan. She began tying cloths around her abdomen and told Sukool that she was pregnant. Obviously, she refused a check-up by midwife. This drama continued for months but the question was, where would she get baby from?

In those days some exorcists using *jhaad-phoonk* would roam in the plantations. Eliza contacted one of them and gave him ten dollars to get her a child. This story is from 1905 on the Melville plantation. That this story would end in such a gruesome manner is beyond imagination.

A pregnant Indian woman named Kishuni was found murdered, with her body found in the sugarcane fields. Her belly was slit and the baby in her womb was stolen. In a few hours from that incident, Eliza gives birth to a dead child simply to prove that she had indeed been pregnant.[9]

Tale of bold Baby

Whatever her actual name may have been, on the Demerara Island she was known as Baby. She was illegally married off by her *Girmitiya* parents at the age of 12. After six months of her marriage, her lover Tallu made her elope with him. Tallu was ten years older than her and they grew up together in the *Girmitiya* barracks. He worked in Georgetown with Inspector Francis. Tallu gave Baby many expensive gifts and jewellery.

Subsequently, one Lt. Alexander fell in love with Baby. He wanted to elope with Baby to Suriname or Venezuela. However, he could not carry out his plans because Tallu came to know of it. When Tallu came to look for her, she wasn't with Alexander but with an Indian named Dedideel. Tallu was heartbroken. He realised that Baby was not somebody who would remain tied with one lover. With the help of a police officer friend, Tallu took away all the jewellery he has gifted to her and tore her skirt in rage. Dedideel came to her rescue but couldn't put up a fight.

At last, they had to go to the police station and compromise, but over there Alexander sided with Baby. Surprisingly enough Baby went missing again. This time she ran away to Suriname. Probably this arrangement was the planned by Alexander. She came back only once to meet her mother.

In these years there were five men in Baby's life, and she made them all dance to her tune.[10]

Gladstone Coolies

British Guyana is a beautiful country at the northern tip of Southern America. Anyone can get lost in the dense rainforests here. This country, surrounded by rivers, is not exactly an island although it looks like one. The neighbouring Dutch Guyana is now known as Suriname. British brought *Girmitiyas* to Guyana for themselves and to sell some of them to the Dutch. I shall discuss the Sarnami Indians of Suriname later in the book. Let's focus on Guyana or British Guyana or Demerara, the abode of most *Girmitiya* descendents in West Indies.

West Indies suffered the maximum losses due to the abolition of slavery. Between 1838 and 1850, 112 companies were shut down. The quality of sugar was deteriorating day by day. The free African slaves refused to listen to the commands of their masters, and often created ruckus. The plantation owners were very worried about this situation. They needed slaves from anywhere or their existence was in danger.[11]

They first tried getting labourers from Europe. Since 90% population were free African slaves, they wished to increase the percentage of Whites there.[12] But who would come from Europe to work on plantations? Still, in the first consignment, about 30,000 labourers were brought from Portugal. A second attempt was made to get black workers from North America and Barbados. But this didn't help much either.

Guyana was the highest producer of sugar in West Indies due to their hard work and their competitive spirit. John Gladstone was the father of the British Prime Minister William Gladstone. He had two big plantations in Guyana--Vreid-en-hoop and Vreid-en-stein. When slavery was abolished in America, he wrote a letter to an agent in Calcutta – Glanders Arbuthnot who were already sending people to Mauritius and Reunion. On 5th May 1838, 396 labourers set off for Guiana (now Guyana); they were taken on two ships, viz. *Whitby* and *Hesperus*. They were called the Gladstone Coolies. In the first few ships, the *Girmityas were* from the Chhota Nagpur Plateau region. They were called 'Hill coolies' or *Dhangars*. These Uranv and Munda tribal people were well-built, especially in comparison with people from Bihar and UP. On the first ship itself about 150 *Dhangars* arrived. Between 1845 and 1848, half the labourers who arrived were from Madras and half from Bengal. During the entire *Girmitiya* period, about 80% of the total 500,000 workforce were from India. About 300,000 of them were for British Guyana alone.

In the beginning when these labourers came here, they began to devise means of running away. From a plantation named Belle View, twenty labourers ran away in a boat. But where would they go? It was impossible to reach India on boat. A few days later they were found starving in the forests of a nearby island.[13] *Madrasi* labourers would always shirk work and try to run away from the plantations, but the labourers from Bengal were disciplined and hardworking. Probably Madras labourers had come from urban settlements and those from Bengal had come from villages. According to the report by Dr. Bunyan, 1249 (33.5%) of the total 3985 Tamil labourers had died or run away in 1845, whereas only 265 labourers out of 3668 from Calcutta ran away. Those who ran away would often go to Georgetown or New Amsterdam and worked as grass-cutters, cowherds or as fishermen.

The *Madrasis* were somewhat wild in nature. They would roam about here and eat anything they found. They would even pick up animals rotting in garbage and eat them after cooking. However, there were two kinds of people among them too. The first were untouchables and uncouth. The second was somewhat more civilised. But in the context of hygiene, labourers from Calcutta were overall better.

From the 396 Gladstone coolies who had arrived in the first few years, 236 people returned to India by 1843. They took back about 5296 pounds with them. Nearly a 100 people had died during the five years of their contract period while 60 people stayed alive in Guyana. In 1857, 385 people had boarded the ship *Merchantman*. More than a hundred had died on the way and the corpses were thrown into the sea. The rest became sick and only ten people were fit after the journey. Initially, ships took about 96 days to reach, which later became 41 days long.[14]

Conditions in the plantations were so deplorable that the local magistrate Charles Anderson wrote a complaint about it, but it was hushed up. Not only plantation owners but even the Church wanted labourers to be brought here. The government also realised that getting Chinese labourers from Malacca and African labourers from Sierra Leone wasn't easy. On one hand there was economic loss and on the other, moral downfall. Economy proved to be more crucial than morality.

There are some instances of revolt on the ships too. Some prisoners of 1857 revolt in India had been made to board the ship *Classmodern* in 1862. They were already a rebellious lot. They revolted on the ship saying that the journey was taking longer than what they were told. Finally, the ship had to be docked in Pernambuco in Brazil.[15]

Steps on the land of Guyana

When these labourers reached Guyana, it was extremely hot to live there and work in the fields. Fortunately, in the beginning, the rules weren't so strict. People had permission to go outside the plantation. Many labourers in the initial days would run away and never return to work. Later, rules were made stringent. In 1852 when agent Thomas Kerd reached Calcutta, he sang exaggerated praises of the plantations in West Indies and Mauritius. He asserted that the conditions were excellent. Agreement to these places was thus extended to ten years, which included five years of contractual labour. One could return only after ten years. But what agent Thomas didn't tell the truth

"Each day is becoming tougher Saheb. One cannot make ends meet with this much money. Our stomachs don't fill," said Kjol, a leader of the labourers.

Most Indian labourers were put to work on sugarcane plantations, but some were also sent to coconut and coffee plantations. According to the Cummins report of 1891, 600 labourers out of ten thousand labourers worked in coconut and coffee plantations. But by nineteenth century, many Indian labourers were sent to these plantations, especially when demand for coffee increased.

Every morning there would be a muster roll, names were called out. The labourers who reached slightly late, their wages were deducted, and they were made to work for free that day. Those who came on time but didn't work properly, their wages were deducted. If anyone protested, they were jailed. In 1863 in Georgetown Jail, out of the 4900 people imprisoned, 3100 were Indian labourers. In the twenty years between 1874 and 1894, 65,000 Indians were punished.

Later, labourers needed a pass from the manager to step out of the estate/plantation. Very often, they would either lose this pass or by mistake step out of the boundaries of the estate. The punishment was imprisonment. The prohibition on roaming was also to prevent then negotiating wages with another plantation worker. *Sardars* would also take bribes for issuing passes. When police would catch them outside without a pass, they would take a bribe too. So, if one had money, it was not difficult to run away.

In the barracks, the labourers from Madras and Bengal were forced to stay together but there was almost no possibility of any mutual understanding between them, and the root cause of this was language. Both the groups could not understand each other's language. They all learnt to speak in broken English to communicate with each other. The two groups often broke out into fights. If one group would go on strike, the other did not support them. But gradually, over the years, the conflicts were resolved.

The labourers would get a daily wage of 24 cents but initially this wasn't regular. It was regularized 24 years after the first ship arrived in 1862.[16] Many labourers would earn 28 cents every day on an average whereas as per a report (1895), but about 40% labourers would get 12 cents or less. Why wouldn't they be given wages as per the contract? In a plantation called Yohana Cecilia, a labourer named Govinder died of starvation because he would just get 8 cents per day. In 1897 a labourer named Bechu even put a petition separately in front of the Royal Commission that he was not getting any money. In some of the plantations, wages would be withheld for a week and sometimes even for a month. All this was the owner's discretion.[17] The agent-general James Crosby, was quite popular among the labourers between 1858 and 1880. He was so popular that even the agent who came after him was called Crosby. He would openly support the labourers but reaching out to him wasn't easy.

There was one advantage they had in the plantations of Guyana; they were allowed to keep cows. Gradually Indians established control over the milk supply to the villages around the estate. This was an additional income for them.

After returning to India, some labourers narrated a strange experience. In 1851 *Madrasi* people who returned in the ship *Zenobia* around 1851 reported that a strange type of worm *Jigga* was entering the body and if not treated early, limbs needed to be amputated.They warned the people to not go to Demerara. This scared many of the new labourers going there.

Women of Guyana

Plantation owners preferred married women and widows. According to them these women were hard working. Unmarried lower caste women were called *randi* (whore) in the estates. Many marriages were solemnised at the depot itself and couples often agreed because they were told that it was easier to find a job if they were married. However, there were some instances where both parties refused to acknowledge the marriage after boarding the ship. In 1883 on board the ship *Rohilla,* a Nepali woman Moti refused to acknowledge Aburber as her husband.[18] In 1886 on board the ship *Phayl*, a woman named Aseram came to the depot with her husband Aladdin. She took his protection but did not sleep with him. As soon as she alighted from the ship, she asked to be sent to another plantation as she didn't consider Aladdin her husband.[19]

In the initial ships *Whitby* and *Hesperu*s, there was a small number of women. Of the 400 people aboard, only 25 were women including 11 girl children. Next year, an eight-year-old girl Nunnidi was raped and killed. It is only after such brutal incidents that focus was turned on to increasing the number of women there.[20] First the quota of women labourers was four women for every ten men which was increased to 50% in 1863. It was difficult to maintain this ratio. Many men would not travel with their wives. Wives were either left behind in the village or the men were single. Single women were more in number. They also had their own stories; most of them had run away from the stifling social milieu of India.

Several Chinese *Girmitiyas* too boarded these ships, but the Chinese consignment consisted only of men. The Chinese initially stayed away from the Indians but gradually with no other option they started having relationships with the Indian women. They found them more attractive than the African women. In 1892, six Chinese men married Indian women. Some took them back to China, but it is difficult to trace them now. Indian men too did not want to marry African native women. There are instances of some European landowners having sexual relations with Indian women.

Just like other islands, women in Guyana earned less wages and got less food than the men. Their work was more assistive in nature than primary. Older or mature women looked after the children and were called *Khelauni*. They were the ones who inculcated basic Bhojpuri language among children.

Misbehaving with women was common in the barracks but reached its peak when a husband came to know about the extramarital affairs of his wife Laungi. He beat her, threw her on the ground and with a broken glass bottle hurt her so badly that she bled profusely. When she tried to run out of the house, he dragged her back and chopped off her toes. She was taken to the hospital, but she died due to excessive blood loss. When a case was filed against him, the judge said that probably he had acted as per the rules of his native country and rightly so. Just before he was hanged to death, he prayed *Hey Ram*, perhaps to attain salvation.

The influence of Lord Rama and *Ramcharitmanas* was immensely present in Guyana. After work, there would be Ramcharitmanas recitals in the evening. Coolies tried to search for Rama in themselves. They thought that they are also in an exile like Ram and are roaming in the forests and their wives were like Sita for them. So, whoever tried to dishonour them was Ravana to them. If her character was in question, then like Surpnakha her nose could be cut off as punishment. A man named Muti cut the nose of his lover Maharayi. Kalyan Singh killed his mistress Umrayi.

Lacchminiya was seven months pregnant and Ramavatar was unable to bear her expenses. Hence she had begun to live with another

Girmitiya named Bheekhu. In a fit of anger, Ramavtar slit his wife Lacchminiya's throat in the field and began shouting, "I have killed a whore! I have killed a whore!"

The poor man possessed only one shirt which was soaked in blood. He was sentenced to death, but he had no regret. This kind of justice became a norm in Guyana in the first half of the nineteenth century itself. Between 1859 and 1917 husbands or lovers killed 167 women!

Local government enacted many laws to lessen such incidents. But the Indian mindset was such that they weren't scared of even death sentence. They held their honour dearer than their life. Whiplashes or other punishments also failed to deter such incidents. When a manager suspected such an incident, they would transfer the person to another plantation. In 1860 an ordinance was passed that if someone stole another man's wife, there would be a fine of 24 dollars and if the offence was repeated, the fine would be 100 dollars. But this was applicable only when the marriage was legal. Generally, the marriages weren't registered according to British laws and hence these fines were not meted out. As per the statistics in 1893, there were 1,10,000 Indians in Guyana, out of which only 10,000 Indians held a marriage certificate.

There are some other tales too. Like, an Indian man shared his wife with a Chinese man because his Chinese friend, was lonely and wanted to have a child of his own. The woman who shared bed with these two men was nicknamed later as 'Gang-Gang'.[21]

Many women who could not bear children committed suicide. They had come from a culture where it was crucial to have an heir. Only a son could cremate his father. In a *Girmitiya's* life even if she was fertile, bringing a pregnancy to term wasn't easy. Often there would be stillbirths that forced the mother to kill herself. Husbands would often abandon these women. That is why women who were already mothers were highly in demand because they were considered capable of bearing children.

Casteism in Guyana

About 83% people here spoke Bhojpuri or Awadhi, most of them were from Uttar Pradesh or Bihar. Although there were people from Bengal,

Orissa, Jharkhand, Andhra, Tamil Nadu, and Punjab as well. About 85% were Hindus and 15% Muslims.

Caste Division

1. *Khetihar*/Peasants (*Dhanuk, Kurmi, Koiri, Ahir)* – 30%
2. Dalit (*Chamar, Dom, Dusadh*) 25%
3. *Savarna* (*Brahmin, Bhoomihar, Thakur*) – 11%
4. *Kumhara, Badhai* – 9%
5. *Madrasi*- 3%
6. *Baniya*- 2%
7. *Pahadi Coolie/Tribal* – 2%
8. *Mallah*- 2%
9. *Vaishya*- 1%
10. *Others*- 5%

The proportion of Hill coolies (*Dhangar*) could have been more in the initial twenty years when more than half were *Dhangars*. But their documents were not kept with care and later with time they became irrelevant for the other *Girmitiyas*. They were tribals and their lifestyle was different. It is possible that they mingled better with the Africans. Some sources assert that *Dhangars* died in large numbers on the ships and plantations. They could never settle down there properly. They stopped coming after 1860; however, in the last few years a small group of Hill Coolies did come.

Europeans were careful not to assign bigger responsibilities to Brahmins. They found them clever and deceitful. Pathans and Punjabis were also not kept together on one plantation. They were believed to be aggressive people. There were allegations on Brahmins and Kshatriyas that they behaved like self- styled leaders and cajoled people to give away their money to them. There were a few incidents where they would take the new labourers to a deserted spot and tell them that the road would lead to India. They would then snatch away their money and leave them there to die.[2] There is a mention of a person called Lal Singh who did such act.[23] Later many dead bodies and skeletons were found in these forests and sugarcane fields.

In another incident, an upper caste woman married a lower caste man and after returning to India, she took away all his money and abandoned him. The poor fellow returned to West Indies with the help of an agent and pledged never to marry an upper caste woman. According to Dr. Cummins' memoir, an upper caste man abandoned his lower caste wife and children as soon as they reached Calcutta.

After many years of doing collective *Girmitiya* labour, caste system has weakened here. Now a *Chamar* or an untouchable from the South may have more wealth than a *Kshatriya*. One didn't have to be a *Baniya* to open a shop. But Indians held a belief that the black Africans were an inferior race than them and so relationship with them was not encouraged. But there were exceptions. In 1842 a child born of such relationship between an Indian and African unfortunately did not survive.[24]

Rebellion of the *Girmitiyas*

After 1860, many rules were flouted often. Labourers made organizations and began to go on strikes. In July 1869, the largest strike in those times happened at the Leonora plantation (West Coast of Demerara). In that plantation, the work could not be completed due to the wet soil but their wages were cut. Labourers went on strike and asked for a raise. The next year, there were strikes in six more plantations. Local police and military had to be sent to break the strikes. However, this resistance paid off and wages were raised.

The second biggest rebellion was in the plantations of Devonshire Castle in 1872. Here labourers raised issues like long working hours, strange division of work, and less wages. This time the police opened fire and five labourers were killed and many were injured.

Around 1896 there is mention of a person named Junglee in the Nanparel Plantation. Junglee had participated in the revolt of 1857 in India as a soldier. When he was thrown out of the army, he came to work in Guyana. The deputy manager of plantation cast his eyes on his wife. Sometime later, she began to live with him as his mistress. This was enough to make Junglee's blood boil. He gathered the other labourers and initiated an organised rebellion. But this rebellion was crushed, and five labourers were killed.

In May 1903 there was an organised rebellion in a plantation named Friends where hundreds of *Girmitiyas* protested to get their wages raised. But police opened fire killing six people and injuring seven. But they didn't accept defeat and they continued strike. When warrants for their arrest were issued, they were ready to go to prison.

In Rosehall revolt of 1913, fifteen lives were lost and 39 people were injured. This was the most horrific revolt so far. One of the leaders was an educated Maula Baksh who had mentioned the non-fulfilment of the agreement. The news of this revolt reached India and Indian leader Surendra Nath Banerjee took it up in the Viceroy's Legislative Council on 9 September 1913. It was only after this revolt that there was a huge outcry for abolition of the *Girmitiya* tradition. That year itself Gandhi had taken out a huge rally of coolies in Natal. Pressure was mounting on Lord Hardinge, the Viceroy of India.[25]

After *Girmitiya* Era

There were protests from time to time in Britain too regarding the abolition of the *Girmitiya* tradition. The "Anti-slavery Society" of London raised its voice against the oppression of the Gladstone coolies, In India, the Congress and the Muslim League jointly passed a bill against the *Girmitiya* tradition. Purushottam Das from Bihar and Arya Samaji Swami Satya Dev who made fiery speeches in Darbhanga and Muzaffarpur.[26]

When *Girmitiyas* became free, they had several options before them. If they had saved enough money, they returned to India. When the contract of the first hill coolies got over in 1842, all of them wanted to go back to India. It is evident that their life must have been very difficult, and they had been waiting for this day. Plantation owners tried to convince them to stay back but they didn't agree. When their rations were stopped, they sat on a hunger strike. They just wanted to return to India at any cost. But, the trends changed later.

Till 1918, a total of 3,41,600 labourers were sent to Guyana. Only 75,000 returned. There were many reasons behind this. Many of them had inter-caste marriages and were sure to be expelled from their community after returning to India. Some didn't have enough savings to pay the dues of the landlords back home. Some were already banished from the society due to the notion of *Kaala Paani*. The best option was to stay back and work on the sugar plantations as free workers. Here they had free shelter, free rations, free healthcare, and a small plot of their own. Those who didn't want to work under anyone could also buy their own plot of land and do farming. Many craftsmen started their own business. Some opened small shops. Some went to the city and took up a job. A few of them went out of West Indies towards North and South America. It is difficult to find details of all of them because there are no records after the expiry of the contract. One person returned to India in 1869 with 10,000 dollars and opened a big store and later became a rich merchant. But usually, it was impossible to save such a large amount of money. Between 1871 and 1910, majority of the *Girmitiyas* were so poor that they had to be sent back to India on government expenses.[27]

In 1880 the land of Huist Derren plantation in Guyana was divided into plots and given to the *Girmitiya* people by the government. Each adult was given about a quarter and two acres of land, a child worker between ten and fifteen years was given two acres, and children less than ten years were granted half an acre. When this scheme was stopped, the plots were sold at twenty-four dollars per acre. But Indians found cheaper land at five dollars per acre somewhere else and moved there.[28] Later, in 1897, the scheme was revived again for five years. But the government began to believe that rather than giving them free land, it was better to make them capable to buy some land themselves.

It was common for Indians to go job hunting to the city of Georgetown, but they invariably came back disappointed. They would often sleep on roadsides, defecate in the open and thus ridiculed. After doing some odd jobs they would return to the village. In those days, one Englishman named Alexander helped them. One morning, he had an epiphany that he was born to protect these poor Indian coolies. He changed his name to *Garibdas* and started wearing Indian attire. He set up an inn near the Demerara coolie depot where he lodged and fed poor coolies or those who had run away and come to the city. But such Messiahs of the poor were few.[29]

After freedom from contract, that majority of the Chinese took to business while Indians continued to do farming. Agriculture was their strength. Farmers from Bihar- UP had experience of wheat farming. *Ahirs* had experience with cattle. Soon the responsibility of supplying grains and fruits to the entire West Indies was taken over by the Indians. Indians started producing more than the black natives of Guyana. They started their separate business of sugarcane farming, wheat farming, fishing, and dairy. Indian tailors and potters too were in demand.

However, it is incorrect to say that Indians began wheat farming in West Indies. It was the slaves coming from West Africa who started cultivating wheat here first, followed by the people from Sierra Leon and Liberia. But the contribution of making wheat a major crop in Guyana lies entirely with the Indians. Till 1884 Guyana imported 19,411 tonnes of rice but by 1916 Guyana began to export it.[30] With time, sugarcane farming began to decline and rice cultivation began to rise. By 1917 Guyana had 86 rice mills. Also 80% of the milk in Guyana was in the control of Indians. In 1893 one Indian had seven hundred cows![31]

Religion in Guyana

Girmitiyas practised Hinduism based on their memories and is thus different from what is practiced in India. Later many proponents of Hindu religion came from India and hence the religious methods kept changing. Islam was also largely successful in maintaining its identity. There was immense pressure to convert to Christianit, but Indians considered Christianity inferior and didn't agree to convert readily. Chinese and Africans on the other hand, easily adopted Christianity. For Hindus, their religion was deeply entrenched in their blood. They kept statues of Hindu gods and goddesses in their homes. Muslims also performed Namaz and followed Muslim traditional rituals. When they became free, they began to do all this in an organised manner.

In the later years many Indians got attracted towards Christianity, more so when they became prosperous and modern. They began to learn and speak English. Their children were sent to English medium schools and their interactions with the Africans grew. Gradually they began to lose their Indianness. The missionary propaganda done by priest J.W. Cropper in 1896 was a major contributor in this, although only a few Indian children would go to his school in the beginning. They Indians were not too inclined to study, fearing that their children would be converted. Canadian missionary schools changed this perception. They would teach for free and give away books in both English and Indian languages. This attracted the children, and many children were sent to missionary schools. Although, in 1913 only about 25% of Indian children were literate, whereas among the blacks the literacy rate was about 85%.[32]

There were, however, several people active towards saving Hindus from the Christian missionaries. Especially, a handful Brahmins had taken the lead in this. This is explained thus in this folk song-[33]

"We bow our heads to the Brahmin who narrates the tale
who teaches us prayers, Sandhya and Havan
Obeisance to the Brahmin who makes temples here
He saves all those, led astray by the mission."

(Re-Translated)

Fagwa (Holi) is most popular in Guyana. *Chautals* written by a Brahmin *Girmitiya* Lal Bihari Sharma, are still sung. Especially, I was mesmerised when I listened to this *Chautal* sung by Amar Ramesar:[34]

Ulara:

My lover, the grandson of the white-bearded man
When I talk, he doesn't talk
Ogling at others with swagger walk
My lover, the grandson of the white-bearded man.

Chautal:

Friend! Get up, let's groom for the spring
Bracelets, bangles and let's paint our nails
Wear the beaded necklace which suits, and the favourite dot on head |1|
Ornamented sitting on the bed, crying oh lover!

I'm longing, he doesn't listen, my youth forces me |2|
My blouse tightens, while my body trembles in desire
Sexual longing is unbearable, and worry weans my body |3|
Oh lover! Sings the cuckoo, but I don't have any patience
Lal Bihari sympathises, Lady! Please stay patient |4|

It is ironic that despite being in the American continent, patriarchal system exists even now.[35] Arranged marriages are still prevalent among Hindu families in countryside. In many cases the groom, a Guyana Indian may be settled in America.

Their language is a chutney of Bhojpuri and Creole. Though these people have never set foot in India, they carry it in their heart even today. Gaiutra Bahadur remembers in her book that in Guyana in her village's cinema hall, the Hindi film *Love Story* Kumar Gaurav was screened.[36]

'Indian Arrival Day' is celebrated on 5th May every year.

Indian dishes like *Daal-poori*, *Parsad* (dessert made of coconut powder), chicken curry, Gulab Jamun and Kheer is very popular in Guyana. *Girmitiyas* had also brought some seeds and plants like Okra (lady finger) and different Ayurvedic leaves along with them. Especially women had brought plenty of sunflower seeds.

Their children began to take a lot of interest in cricket and the West Indian team began to challenge teams like England and Australia. Guyana was now Indians' playground. Alvin Kaalicharan, Rohan Kanhai, Shiv Narayan Chandrapaul, Ramnares Sarwan and Mark Rampraksha of *Girmitiya* descendence are some well-known cricketers from Guyana.

Indians in Politics

Guyana has about 3,50,000 Indians who constitute about 43% of their population. Cheddi Berret Jagan was the fourth President of Guyana and is also known as the Father of the Nation. In 1901 his father Jagan along with his mother Jagaoni, his two grandmothers and two uncles were brought here from Uttar Pradesh. His father was a labourer in the sugarcane fields, and Cheddi Jagan was the oldest among 11 siblings. He witnessed the *Girmitiya* struggle from close quarters though his father put him in an English school. Later he also trained to be a dentist in America. Jagan was initially a communist, and CIA kept conspiring against him. Later he became more of a socialist. His wife Janet Jagan also became President. Other than Cheddi Jagan and Janet Jagan, Bhagat Jagdeo and Donald Ramotar have been Presidents of Guyana, and Mozez Nagamuthu has been the Prime Minister.

One issue that cropped up in Guyana and rest of the West Indies was the conflict with the native blacks. Indians refused to be categorised as black. Many Indians claimed to be of Caucasian origin and a better race. They would call the natives apes, whereas the African natives would insultingly call them coolies. This conflict began to rise in the decades before the 70s, as the Indian community population increased. There were many attacks like arsons, murder and rapes on Indians in the 70s. This racist violence and was spurred after the removal of Cheddi Jagan and dictator Linden Burnham coming to power. Many Indians migrated to USA after these incidents. But, The *Girmitiyas* of Guyana kept getting better in terms of social status and their future generations grew proud of their ancestors. Rajkumari Singh, a Guyanese Indian said this about the word "coolie" that they hated-[37]

"Adopt this word. Identify with this word. Say proudly that we are coolies."

When India became independent

112 years after the first *Girmitiya* stepped in Guyana the last *Girmitiya* ship set sail for India. The ship was named *Resurgent*. Now that India attained freedom, the *Girmitiyas* wanted to see their free country. Many Guyana born youth and children had never stepped on the Indian soil. Many had a wish to die in their homeland.

But did India want to accept them back? In British Guyana this news was spread that there was no place was for them in India. But for the *Girmitiya* it was still a scared place. All Indians of Guyana and

Trinidad came to see that ship, bid farewell to the travellers. It was an emotional scene. Those on this ship would go to India, those on the ground shall forever live in Guyana. When the ship moved, one person jumped off it, probably because he couldn't leave Guyana either. There were many people like him who had no wish to return to India.

When the ship reached the 'mad sea' of Africa, their decades-old fear returned. Waves were crashing forcefully against the ship and it was shaking violently. When the ship reached Calcutta the Ghat had changed. Now instead of the depot there were the camps of the refugees from East Pakistan (now Bangladesh.) The pain of partition was still afresh but for the *Girmitiyas* who had returned after decades all this was difficult to comprehend. *Girmitiyas* were unwelcome guests

People sitting all the way in Guyana listened to Pandit Jawahar Lal Nehru on All India Radio. He said-

"Thetars (stubborns) have come."[38] Although I have doubt about this context from Gaiutra Bahadur's book that Nehru could have used these exact words.

Did India not want them back? Or the *Thetar* word was used because in spite all the challenges they finally returned to India? These were just 243 people but a country already facing refugee problem could have considered them stubborn to return at such critical times.

V.S. Naipaul found a woman in an Indian village in 1962 who spoke Caribbean language. She had been accepted by the villagers.[39] But this must not have been the case for all. Especially what happened to those who had not returned with some money? They were called *Tapuha*. In many villages they were not allowed to smoke the Hukkah with others. They were not allowed to fill water from the wells of the village. The conditions in which they had returned to a free country were even worse than the ones in which they had left. A child who went to an English school in Guyana now worked as a child labourer in a matchbox factory in Calcutta. Once again, he had become a coolie in India like his ancestors.

The situation was such that many people started urging the government to send them back to Guyana. A boxer named Bal Govind started boxing in Calcutta to save money for a ticket to Guyana.

He had turned so violent and hurt so many people that finally the government had to send him back to Guyana. About 25 people were sent back to Guyana.[40]

Even today in 356 thick registers in Demerara, the contracts with thumb-impressions/signatures of all *Girmitiya* are kept safe. This credit must be given to the British government for saving all these documents. However, after the departure of the British government, these papers were not kept properly. Many registers got destroyed by termites or due to the damp weather. In the files lying on the floor in record offices there are birth and death records of many *Girmitiyas*. In every piece of these scattered papers there is a *Girmitiya*. There is a person.

References

1. Marina Carter, Voices from Indenture: Experiences of Indian Migrants in the British Empire *(New Historical Perspectives on Migration,* Leicester University Press, 1966.
2. Verene Shepherd, *Maharani's Misery*, University of the West Indies Press, 2002
3. Gaiutra Bahadur, Coolie Woman: The Odyssey of Indenture, Hurst and Company, 2013, Secondary Source
4. Verne Ref. 2
5. David Northrup, *Indentured Labor in the Age of Imperialism, 1834–1922*, Cambridge University Press, 1995
6. Gaiutra, op. cit.
7. Ibid.
8. Ibid.
9. Ibid.
10. Ibid.
11. Carter op. cit.
12. David op. cit.
13. "The Horrible Treatment . Hill Coolies", *The Lancet*, 24 August 1839
14. Shepherd, op. cit.
15. Carter op cit.
6. Ibid.
17. Ibid.
18. Gaiutra op cit.
19. Jeremy Pointing, "The East Indian Women in the Caribbean: Experience, Image and Voice", *Journal of South Asian Literature*, 21(1) 1986, pp. 133-80
20. Shepherd op. cit.
21. Gaiutra op. cit.
22. Carter op.cit..
23. Gaiutra op. cit.
24. Carter op.cit.

25. Gaiutra op.cit
26. Ibid.
27. David op.cit.
28. Carter op.cit.
29. Gaiutra op.cit.
30. Carter op.cit.
31. Ibid.
32. Lalbihari Sharma, *Damra- Faag Bahar*, Self-Published, 1972
33. Gaiutra op.cit.
34. Ibid.
35. Carter op. cit
36. Ashwin Desai and Goolam Vahed, Inside Indian Indenture: A South African Story, 1860 – 1914, HSRC Press, (Secondary Source)
37. Gaiutra op.cit.
38. Ibid.
39. V.S. Naipaul, *Finding the Centre*, Alfred Knoff, 1984
40. Gaiutra op.cit.

Trinidad and Tobago, Caribbean Islands

"Emigration was the vehicle of female emancipation."

– Peter Emmer[1]

Prime Minister's Village

If someone goes to an ancestral Indian village of *Girmitiyas* and asks a villager if they knew where the *Girmityas* were sent to, their answer will be Fiji, or some will say *Chinidad.* Some even don't know whether their ancestors went to Fiji or Trinidad. They just know that they went across the seven seas.

Bhelupur is one such village in the Itarhi block of Buxar. Today this village has many brick-laid roads and *pucca* houses. But in the nineteenth century, there were none of them. Somewhere in this village lived a Brahmin named Ram Lakhan Misra. The reasons for upper caste man like him to sail the ship as girmitiya, must have been dire poverty. On 21 October 1889 on board a ship named *Volga,* Ram Lakhan had set off from Calcutta and landed in Trinidad after a month-long voyage. Whether he was married or married after reaching Trinidad is not clear.

Many decades later, his great granddaughter Kamala returned to the ancestral village in a chopper, surrounded by security personnel. She came with her husband Gregory Bissessar wearing a saree and walked on foot to her uncle Jagdish Misra's house. A green carpet was laid for her on the brick-laid path. Thousands of people had thronged here from far-flung villages to listen to her speech. She could't speak Hindi or Bhojpuri fluently.

She said in English, "Today your granddaughter has returned to her roots. Whatever she is and whatever she has achieved is because of you. Your granddaughter is now the Prime Minister of a country."

What could her poor extended family give her? She returned with a few sarees, some sweets and loads of blessings. I wonder if Ram Lakhan had not gone to Trinidad, what would have been the fate of Kamala. India has progressed so much but what is the condition of the women of Bhelupur after 150 years?[2]

Bhagwan Di

Bhagwan Di is her name in the record. A middle-aged married woman who had run away from her home in some village in Bihar. She reached Calcutta via the recruitment depot in Bihar. In 1885 she boarded the ship *Narbuddha* from Calcutta to Guyana.

Bhagwan Di was attractive as well as an extrovert woman. On board she fell in love with a *Sardar* (leader.) Women mostly tried to attract Sardars to get some favours. *Sardars* themselves chased many women. Or maybe Bhagwan Di experienced true love. The thought of runaway married woman falling in love on board a ship in those times is romantic. But something else was in store in Bhagwan Di's fate.

The ship's environment was stressful, and it was difficult to judge somebody's character there. One night she had an argument with the *Sardar,* and he stabbed her in the back with a spear. What happened after that is not clear. Whether the bleeding injured woman tried to run away, or the *Sardar* dragged her body. As per the records, Bhagwan Di took her life by jumping off the ship. The *Sardar* was arrested as soon as he reached Trinidad and imprisoned.[3]

From one Hell to Another

Maharani didn't remember when her parents passed away. She just remembered that when she was five, she sat on her uncle's lap and an old man was sitting with him. While she heard sacred chants and folk songs, garlands were being exchanged. Maharani was getting married to that old man. When Maharani was twelve, her husband died.

Now she was a child widow, dependent on her husband's family. One day her brother-in-law took her to a magistrate and got her thumb impression to take away all her land ownership rights. Thus, she became a servant in her own house, being beaten and punished for every small mistake. One day as she was boiling milk, when a cat toppled the vessel. She got scared that she would be beaten again. This was the moment that changed Maharani's life. She ran away.

She met a crippled man who asked if she would like to go to an island to sieve sugar? She would get twenty-five cents every day. Maharani was in such a miserable mental condition that without thinking she said 'yes'.

At the age of 20 in 1916 Maharani set sail from Calcutta to Trinidad. When she was boarding on to their ship *Chenab,* there was another ship beside full of Girmitiyas returning from Trinidad. Those people were gesturing and signalling her not to go to the island. But their voices were drowned by the loud sound of the ship's horn. It was too late. Maharani was happy. What worse could happen? Anything would be better than her previous life. She remembered seafarers singing and beating *dhol* (percussion instrument like drum). This was the happiest journey of her life. Her path to freedom.

Maharani was asked to have relations with a *Girmitiya* named Ramghoolam, but she wished to live alone. Ramghoolam asked the overseer to intervene, who tried to convince Maharani, but she was adamant. Besides, she considered Ramghoolam an immoral man. At the overseer's behest, Ramghoolam forcibly took her with him. He drugged her to have physical relations with her. Maharani kept denying this forced relationship while her husband continued to sleep with other women. He beat her every day. She conceived nine children with Ramghoolam, five of them died. One day Maharani died too. Whether in India or abroad, her life remained hell.[4]

Queen of Sheeba

According to a myth, the Queen of Sheeba had travelled a long distance to meet Solomon, the king of Jerusalem. She brought along with her spice-laden camels, gold ornaments, diamonds, and gems. When she met the king, they had many polemic discussions. When the king passed her test, she gave him all the wealth and returned.

One such mysterious woman is also described by Captain Angel on board the ship *Sheela* that left India. She gave her the name -- Queen of Sheeba. She was about forty years old confident woman, always well-dressed wearing a lot of jewellery. Among all the women on the ship she was the only one who was full of joy. She had spent some time as a *Girmitiya* even before Trinidad. She earned all her prosperity from there, returning this time not as a Coolie but as a queen.

She loved the island and its people. Most probably she married there and enhanced further her prosperity on the island. When she returned to India, she probably indulged in polemic discussions like women's rights, casteism and *Kaala Paani*, just like Queen of Sheeba. But in a there was no King Solomon there.

She remarked, "This is the country of slaves".

Disappointed she returned to Trinidad with all her wealth.[5]

Women Seafarer, sex-worker

Sukhiya was a sex-worker in Calcutta. But when she boarded the ship *Foyle* in 1889 from Calcutta, she left that life behind her. But history never leaves us.

She met an acquaintance named Roochha on board the ship, who asked her sex for ten dollars. Being a professional prostitute, it was the deal she was used to. He provided him paid sex. But Roochha turned into a jealous lover.

One day he saw a *Sardar* giving Sukhiya a biscuit and he grew suspicious. Biscuit was the secret code for proposing sexual relations on the ship, and accepting it meant consent. This might sound illogical that for a few biscuits women would sell their body, but this was one of the despicable facts on ships.

One night when Sukhiya woke up she saw Roochha in her bed. She didn't know how he had managed to scale the wall between male and female cabins. He could have bribed one of the guards or drilled throught fences. Sukhiya got scared and shouted for help. Next evening when she was sieving rice with some women, Roochha touched her back. Later she alleged that Roochha had touched her breasts as well. In Roochha's eyes she was still a sex worker and that for ten dollars he had bought her body forever.[6]

Girmitiyas of Trinidad

"Where will you take me?"

"*Chinidad*"

"To do what?"

"*Chini chaalne* (Sieving sugar)"

Trinidad is a tiny country comprising a group of five islands with swaying coconut and palm trees and a sandy seacoast where you can find children playing cricket. This is the country of the cricketer Brian Lara. Here the largest leatherback turtles come to lay eggs. So, did many Indian laboureres come here to sieve sugar.

After the slaves were freed, the economy of Trinidad came to a standstill. Between 1847 and 1850 about 40 plantations had shut down.[7] By 1860 in the seven sugar-producing districts of Trinidad, sugarcane production had completely stopped. They badly needed cheap labour from outside.

On 30 May 1845 the first ship *Fatel Razack* arrived at Trinidad carrying 225 bonded labourers from India. Between 1874 and 1917 a total of 1,34,118 people were brought here out of whom 6000 were *Madrasis* (Tamil). In the beginning this voyage used to be three months long, but with the opening of the Suez Canal in 1869 this duration was reduced. In 1917 the last ship *SS Ganges* arrived and after that the arrival of *Girmitiyas* stopped.

As soon as these *Girmitiyas* alighted, they were housed on the Nelson Island. They were told the soil of this place was better than that of India, and they bowed with respect to this new soil. The protector of immigrants would do a cursory check-up. There was always danger of measles and chickenpox coming from India since vaccination was not available. Their blankets and bodies would be disinfected. When it was ascertained that they were free of any disease they were sent to Port of Spain. Those who fell sick were sent to the Colonial Hospital of Port of Spain.

The *Girmitiyas* had to work for five years to work in different plantations and at the completion of five years received a Freedom Certificate. After five years, plantation owners would tempt them with some land and stop them from going back. Majority chosed to stayed back. One condition for going back on government expense was that they had to spend five more years on the island. They were free to work wherever they wanted to but could go back only after ten years. After staying for ten years, they kind of settled down there and lost the desire to return.

Barracks and Plantations

The conditions on Island were like all other *Girmitiya* barracks. Here also they had ten feet long and ten feet high rooms as barracks. The partition in the rooms didn't reach the ceiling hence there was lack of privacy. There was no separate kitchen and food had to be cooked outside on the stairs. Water an hygiene were two main issues here.

Although some barracks had water pumps and wells, but the facilities of water storage were scanty in the barracks. The responsibility of clean water was not taken either by the plantation owners or the labourers. They started drinking water from rivers which further aggravated the problem. Before the twentieth century, there were no toilets and labourers would relieve themselves in the fields. Many outbreaks of epidemics frequently occurred in the barracks, especially malaria, diarrhoea, and cholera. Even if they were ill, they had to work.

Between 1845 and 1848, dead bodies and skeletons of many labourers were found strewn in the fields. These were those labourers who had run from their plantations and died due to starvation. There were many who were unable to work or were afflicted with a serious illness or disease. Between 1847 and 1848, 250 labourers died in the hospital. In 1848, 40 labourers died on a far-off island because the owners did not send food or medicine. In 1851 one labourer was found about 200 miles away from the main island in the faraway tribal areas. How did he manage to reach such a deserted place!

Governor Lord Harris wrote, "In no country of the world was tragedy like the one of these poor, unfortunate labourers experienced due to illness and starvation and finally death."

These labourers would run away from one plantation to another mostly in groups. They hoped of better facilities and lesser work. But this was a mirage. Sometimes it so happened that 50 people ran away from a plantation on a Saturday evening and on Monday morning 50 new people would be standing at the same plantation looking for job![8] Some labourers worked part time in the smaller fields of free Indian farmers.

Many labourers ran away to Venezuela which was barely 25 miles from Port of Spain and the fare in 1876 was 2 dollars. From one part of the island, Venezuela was just 8 miles away where human traffickers ferried them across. Once they reached Venezuela, they were free birds. Wages in the cocoa plantations in Venezuela was better. According to one report, in 1889 about hundred coolies ran away to a place called Güiria in Venezuela. When one family returned from there after several years, they brought along with them a mule and a good amount of money. According to an article by Dr. Cummins, workers travelling to and from Venezuela were often looted and their gold snatched away. In 1897 four Indians were arrested from Venezuela and sent back to their plantation in Trinidad.

To prevent labourers running away from plantations, in 1899 an ordinance (Section 136) was passed that if an immigrant was found wandering in the highway, a ship or in a field not belonging to his master, he would be arrested without any warrant. If he is unable to show the permission letter from the owner, he could be imprisoned by the police.[9] Due to these laws cases of absconding decreased but they didn't stop altogether. Locals were hand in glove with them. One ex- Chief Justice was also arrested as he had given a job to a run-away *Girmitiya* in his house. Apart from run away punishments, abusing a senior, drinking alcohol during work or non-compliance of orders could also lead to deduction of wages. In 1913, after an Indian investigation committee came to Trinidad under the leadership of James McNeill and Chiman Lal, many of these laws were softened.

Indians did make a place for themselves with their hard work, but the owners mostly seemed to be disappointed with them. People of African origin were strong-built, and the work Indians took eight hours to finish they would complete in just four hours. Every year one had to finish 260 tasks on an average, but Indians could only finish about 150. Indians would not come to work every day and did not seem to mind getting their wages deducted or bear the punishment. Many preferred to work for 3-4 days in a week. After 1890 many were absent for about one-third of the time. Plantation owners often persecuted the labourers for this absenteeism. If a labourer missed work for one day, they had to work two extra days in lieu of it. Owing to this rule, the contracts wouldn't end in five years but got stretched to six or seven years.[10] Since it was easier to command the Indian labourers, owners began preferring them over Africans. Gradually, the number of Indian people on the plantations rose and that of African or Creole origin declined.[11] Till 1858 there were about 35% Indians on sugarcane plantations and by 1895 their population rose to 87%! Especially in the Couva area, the percentage of Indians was very high. Another reason for this was Africans didn't want to do menial jobs and preferred doing well paid jobs. The hard work of the Indians labourers paid dividends and income from sugar rose tremendously.[12] Whereas export in 1851 was 2,98,248 pounds, in 1871 it grew to 9,38,000 pounds. This was almost thrice the income from earlier years.[13]

In the initial days there was a magistrate by the name of Major Fegan who was known as the Coolie Magistrate. He supported the coolies a lot and often reprimanded the plantation owners for their harshness towards the coolies. He had even learnt the Hindustani language. He was aghast to see that labourers' clothes were taken away and left to die of starvation on the roads. Many women succumbed to prostitution or died of hunger. Once Major Fegan put three charges on a plantation owner Mr. Walkinshaw who had beaten up a labourer named Bechook mercilessly. On the same plantation another labourer

Kandappa had died due to a wound on his foot. One labourer named Jhandoo told him that they had not received any food for the last five days while they were made to work double shifts. Major Fegan freed all *Girmitiyas* from that plantation and prohibited the further recruitment of any new *Girmitiya* there. In another incident where labourer Bhodu suffered a head injury because of getting beaten, Major Fegan put a strong front against the plantation owner Mr. Anderson. Now, he was becoming cynosure of plantation owners' eyes, and they collectively complained against Major Fegan. There could be one more reason for removing Major Fegan. He had once come to Lord Harris along with 35 *Girmitiyas* and their list of demands. But a British officer leading the labourers was not liked by Lord Harris.[14] He got suspended, but Indians considered him a Messiah. When *Girmitiyas* returned to Calcutta, they spoke highly of him and his sense of justice.[15]

Later came one Thomas Shirley Warner. He also never punished the labourers. People said that even if it was the labourers' fault, he would set nine out of ten of them free. Similarly, one John Gory was also like him. But such kind and just men didn't come often, and labourers remained in a poor state.

Many a times issues wouldn't even reach the courts. Plantation owners employed some henchmen, often *Sardars* or drivers to beat up the poor labourers. Once the manager of Saint Madelyn Estate, Peter Able, tied up Sitaram and five other labourers in the hot sun as punishment. When this information reached the Protector of Immigrants William Coombs, Peter Able had to pay a fine of 60 dollars, 10 dollars for each labourer.

Many labourers did sit on strike now and then, but it remained limited to their plantation. Notable among them was the Harmony Hill strike of 1903, which was the longest and most organised one. Several labourers were sent to jail. One of the leaders of the strike, Daulat Singh, a *Kshatriya,* was sent back to India. Probably some black lawyer was behind this strike.[16] Sometimes protests became aggressive. In 1907 a group of Punjabi and *Madrasi* labourers beat up two *Sardars* to death.

Despite poor conditions, reports from Trinidad were relatively better. When Grierson made queries in the villages of Bihar and Central

Province, more people were interested in going to *Chinidad* (Trinidad) and less to *Damera/Damrella* (Dememara, Guyana). A woman named Gregory Duruti worked in the secretariat at that time. In 1917 when the last ship *SS Ganges* reached there, she arrived with a gramophone and camera to meet them. The labourers from India had never seen such things and were excited to get their pictures clicked. The popular song of Ruddy Vallee, "I ain't got nobody, and nobody cares for me" was playing on the gramophone. Ironically, this was the plight of the *Girmitiyas.*

When the first ship *Eliza Stewart* returned to Calcutta in 1851, the labourers described their experience as good. Many of them wished to return. Not many talked about their torturous existence on the islands. They had brought some money with them. On an average every labourer had about ten pounds in pocket and every *Sardar* about fifty pounds. The only complaint they had was about the *Madrasis,* who according to them, were 'bad people'.[17]

A priest Underhill sums up in his diary-

"Quite possible that some atrocities did take place, but I never heard about any. I am sure that at least people with whom I had relations with would have surely told me then. I travelled to all plantations and saw

Girmitiyas in Trinidad. 1897 (Courtesy- Wikimedia Commons)

it all myself. The huts in which the coolies lived were much better than those in India. People appeared to be eating and living well. I spoke to the people of Bengal, Oudh, and Bihar on plantations. Everybody seemed happy."

Another priest Gambell wrote-

"People's condition was good, and they seemed happy with their families and children. They got a small piece of land where they raised a pig or a cow. They were particularly fond of cows and took good care of them. There were instances when a coolie got beaten up by the driver or the *Sardar*, but this can happen in any country. I would say that coolies improved their lot after leaving the plantations. Not just that, they even got rid of the evil of casteism. The Indians of Trinidad are ready to become Christians now."[18]

A British school teacher in Trinidad wrote that an Indian woman loaded with gold-silver ornaments was returning home with twelve thousand pounds! Even the wives of British farmers weren't so fortunate.[19] But to make such huge savings, Indians lived very frugally and survived on minimum food. When an Indian labourer named Moolchan died in 1878, 12500 pounds were found with him. Quite possibly he had starved himself to save that much money.

Women *Girmitiyas* in Trinidad

One widow along with her five-year old child and a packet of jewellery was wandering aimlessly at a railway station in India looking for way to her paternal village. A stranger told her that he would help her. He robber her and packed her on a train to a depot in Calcutta from where she came to Trinidad.[20] The story was not much different from umpteens of such stories we have already come across.

Sardars often kept *Girmitiya* women as mistresses. Between 1845 and 1888, one doctor complained to Lord Harris that a *Sardar* had impregnated seven women *Girmitiyas*. In 1857 in his statement, one *Girmitiya* Bechu confirmed that labourers are not getting wives because *Sardars* keep them as mistresses. In 1891 labourers beat up the son of a plantation owner named Hilson Christian because he had kept some

Girmitiya women as his mistresses.[21] Many times the situation would get out of hand. In a report by Campbell, sometimes the fault also lay with the women. They would seduce these men so that they didn't have to work much. Between 1872 and 1898, 63 women were killed by their husband due to infidelity.

There were also cross-cultural interactions. Chinese male labourers preferred *Madrasi* women rather than women from Bengal and United Province. Women from North India were from a patriarchal society, hence they were inhibited and scared to marry outside their community, while Tamil women were more liberal minded. Chinese men had come here long before Indians and were prosperous. They attracted them with expensive gifts. It may be possible that relation with Chinese people were considered over Africans, because of their skin colour. There were not many restrictions on sexual relations in the Caribbean Islands, but Africans were often termed *Habsi* (Negro).

After Freedom

In Trinidad, Indians were freed earlier, and they created their influence outside Port of Spain. After 1870 a new rule came into existence that those who did not wish to return to India would get ten acres of land in lieu of their return ticket. People began to accept these ten acres of land and started farming on them. Often, they would take adjacent lands with other Indians. Most of them settled in Ward of Montserrat. They started controlling the dairy business in Trinidad. This could be possible because Indians lived as a tightly knit community there.[22] Richer Girmitiyas preferred to travel to India in superior and expensive ships rather than on cheap *Coolie* ships.

But it wasn't so easy in the beginning as they didn't have much experience of managing a farm, especially after ten years of working as a labourer. Some people were given forest land and they had to cut down the trees to make it cultivable. Others got marshy land near the sea which was unfit for farming. Those who had their own land also worked in the sugarcane farms for some time, but their heart remained in their own land. In one report by Cummins, a labourer was working in a sugarcane farm. After a few hours the same labourer was seen sitting on a mare in his faraway farm. Managing work at both places is a proof of their hard work, which was a major factor in shaping their bright future there.[23]

Some Indians would rent a piece of road-side land measuring 130 x 70 feet at 10 dollars per annum. There they would build a hut, and rear poultry as well as some cows. Some opened desi liquor (country liquor) shops too. By end of Girmitiya era, about 42% of the shops on the island belonged to Indians. By 1920 Indians had about 95,000 acres of land in which most of the farming was of cocoa. Besides this, sugarcane, maize, coconut, rice, coffee, and fruits were also grown. In an estate in La Brea, Victoria, a man named Budu Singh (a former *Girmitiya*) owned the five hundred acres big Patna Cocoa Estate. His neighbour Bharat Singh had about 200 acres where he grew rice and sugarcane. Rice was the strength of Indians because only they knew how to grow it well. Some even bought some barren lagoon islands and started rice cultivation in those marshy svamps!

Some chose other professions. In 1891, there were 109 Indians who were teachers, including 15 women. These figures are surprising that how after a decade of labour how can someone become a teacher? Possible they were poor learned people from India who came here for money.

Chutney of cultures

At that time there were people of many origins in Trinidad -- French, African, Chinese, Jews, Portuguese, Italian, German, some former slave races. Apart from local Girmitiya Indians, many migrated here from neighbouring islands like Guyana, Jamaica, and Suriname. There was obviously a *chutney* (mix) of cultures.

When Indians began arriving in huge numbers, the locals felt insecure of losing jobs. Descendents of former African slaves thought that the country belonged to them, and Indians were outsiders. C.P. David, an African origin politician protested the *Girmitiya* tradition. Sir Henry Alkazar expressed his concern that it would lead to unemployment in the country. *San Fernando Gazette* and *New Era* newspapers criticised the Indians.

During the Great Depression, the wages of the *Girmitiyas* were reduced while work was increased. Many African origin people became unemployed. In Port of Spain itself about 8000 people were starving on the road. In such circumstances, hatred for Indians grew further.[24]

Still, Trinidad is different from many other former *Girmitiya* countries because Indians assimilated well in the local culture and religion here. Canadian missionary schools were influential in Trinidad and in 1893, a college was opened here for the preachers of Christianity. Many Indians became Christian priests. Inspite of such schools, in 1913 only 23% of Indians were literate.[25]

Among Indians, 75% were from United Province and 13.5% from Bihar. Today about 50% people of Indian origin are Hindus, 12% Muslims and the rest converts to Christianity. Satya Narayan Maharaj's *Sanatan Dharm* Mahasabha is the largest Hindu organisation in Trinidad, while Chinmaya Mission, Arya Samajis and ISKCON are also active. Fagwa (Holi) is more of a national festival in Trinidad. Diwali and Eid are also popular. One of the police firing incidents in 1884 stopped Muharram processions in this island. Chutney music became a fore-runner of cross-cultural interation with singers like Rakesh Yankaran and Sunder Popo leading the bandwagon.

Although cultural fusion happened, Trinidad did not completely break away from India. In 1930, there was an Indian Club that was in touch with the Indian Congress and supported the freedom movement. In 1935 the Indian film *Bal Joban* was screened here. The Indians in Trinidad named many localities based on the names of places from where they had come. One will find Mathura, Kanpur, Faizabad, Barrackpore, Chander Nagar and Lucknow on the map of this island. Residents of Basti (UP) made Basta Hall.

Kamla Prasad Bissessar who is now (2017) the leader of the opposition, was the first woman Prime Minister here. Apart from another prime minister Basdeo Pandey, Rudra Nath Kapildeo and Sambhu Nath Kapildeo have been influential leaders here. V.S. (Vidhyadhar Surajprasad) Naipaul, one of the greatest writers of Indian origin and has won the Nobel Prize. Cricketers like Sunil Narayan and Darren Ganga made their name in sports.

One will find people eating roti and bhindi *bhujia* for breakfast. *Baingan chokha, kohra tarkari* and *aloo chokha* are also popular. Callaloo is a strange mix of dasheen bush, bhindi and coconut ground together and is like a chutney of all cultures.[26] Indian Trinidadians today don't want to return to India. The fifth-sixth generations of the *Girmitiyas* are distant from Indian culture. But some watch Bollywood movies and read news about India.

In 2017, there were 500,000 people of Indian origin on this island. Indians can travel to Trinidad and Tobago without a visa for three months.

There is a saying still popular in Trinidad "Pick your *Jahaji* bundle and leave."

But not many literally did it ever.

References

1. Peter C. Emmer, *Colonialism and Migration:Indentured Labour Before and After Slavery,* Dordrecht, Martinus Nijhoff Publishers, 1986
2. Faizan Ahmad, Trinidad's 'daughter PM' returns to village in Bihar for an emotional reunion, Times News Network, 12 January, 2012
3. Warren A. Shepherd, *Maharani's Misery*, University of West Indies Press, 2002
4. Gaiutra Bahadur, Coolie Woman: The Odyssey of Indenture, Hurst Company, 2013, (Secondary Source)
5. Ibid.
6. Ibid.
7. Marina Carter, *Voices from Indenture, Experience of Indian migrants in the British Empire*, Leicester University Press, 1966
8. Carte, op.cit.
9. Carter, op.cit.
10. David, op.cit.
11. David Northop, *Indentured Labour in the Age of Imperialism, 18343-1922,* Cambridge University Press, 1995
12. Gerad M.Teeka Singh, The Establishment of Indians in Trinidad, 1870-1900 (Context Bridget Breton's work"Race Relations in Colonial Trinidad") Unpublished research document
13. Ibid.t
14. J.H. Collains, *A Guide to Trinidad: A Handbook for the Use of Tourists and Visitors*, General Books, 2010

15. Carter, op. cit.
16. Hughes Tinker, *New System of Slavery: The Export of Indian Labour Overseas, 1830-1920*, Oxford University Press, London, 1974
17. Carter,op.cit.
18. W.H. Gambell, *Trinidad, Historical and Descriptive, Being a Narrative of Nine Years Residence in Island*, London,1866
19. Collians, op.cit.
20. Gaiutra, op.cit.
21`.Carter,op. cit.
22. Ibid.
23. Ibid.
24. Gerard Besan, *Nelson Island, Caribbean History Archives*, Parriah Publishing (Internet Source)
25. Carter, op. cit.
26. Neel Sukdev, Freedom, *Festivals and Caste in Trinidad after Slavery*, Jhilbris Corporation, 2001

Jamaica and rest of Caribbean

When the capitalism of Britain was fully dependent on West Indies, they didn't care much about the tradition of slavery. But when the monopoly of West Indies began to trouble them, they abolished the slavery and destroyed this monopoly itself.

- Eric Williams[1]

When *Girmit* saved the country

In 18th century half of Europe's sugar came form the West Indies. The traders became reluctant to send sugar to Britain, rather they sold it to other countries at better prices. Their monopoly was growing. One of the reasons for British Prime Minister to abolish slavery, was to curb down this West Indian monopoly!

Adding to their woes, sugar tax was removed in 1846 and Britain began to buy from other countries in stead of West Indies.[2] In 1847-88, Britain went into an economic crisis, and sugar prices plummeted downs. Plantation owners were unable to pay wages to the labourer. The condition turned from bad to worse. Their soil was losing its fertility and production was decreasing. Jamaica was counting its last breaths.

After getting freedom, many Africans began to leave Jamaica abandoning the plantations. They didn't imagine that Indians would come and come in such large numbers that they would become redundant anyway.

Steps in Jamaica

In 1845, first ship Maidstone arrived at Old Harbour Bay. It had 200 men of less than thirty years of age, 28 women and 33 children of less than 12 years. Between 1845 to 1917 a total of 36,000 Indians came to Jamaica, mostly from the states of Rajasthan, Bihar and UP.[3]

At their arrival each of them got a welcome kit, containing a piece of cloth, farming stuff, and one vessel to cook food. They were divided into groups of 20-40 and were taken to the plantations in mule carts or in cargo trains. Their wages were about one shilling per day. They needed to pay two shillings and six pence per month for ration of rice, flour, peas, dried fish, dries mutton and a few spices. Children were given half the rations but they got regular free health check-ups.

Plantation owners in Jamaica lived a lavish life with huge well-furnished British styled bungalow. They had large halls with piano, chandeliers, cozy couches, and paintings on the walls. From the balcony, they could oversee the labourers working in the fields with their binoculars. They would be sipping lemonade while some coolie would be clipping their toenails. They could almost sleep with any *girmitiya* woman they wished to.

They often used to beat the labourers with their shoes and even shot at them with guns. In case of firing, there would be a stampede with labourers running helter-skelter. People would hide in their barracks and peeped from the keyhole if someone was coming towards them. To summarise it, the condition here was miserable. They got lesser wages than European and Africans and were teased as coolies.

Labourers would run away and could be found begging in Kingston. Such runaway beggars carried a bag on their shoulder and would be picking stuffs from garbage. Usually, people coming from rural India worked well in farms. Urban *Girmitiya* from Calcutta would often resort to begging. Probably they were beggars back there too. They would stand for hours outside windows with a face devoid of emotions and dried off eyes.[4]

There are reports of conflict between *Madrasi* and Bihari labourers. As soon as they alighted from the ship *Deva* in 1917, some argument broke out in which 17 people were injured.[5] North Indians considered *Madrasi* people useless. Owners also preferred Bengali and Bihari labourers. *Madrasi* were kept as domestic servants or cooks.[6]

After five years of bonded labour, government offered them land or money to sustain their lives. Fearing that they would get land on a barren mountain, most of them chose money. Many of them worked as construction workers for Panama Canal in 1884.

Bob Marley and Indians

Jamaica has about 100,000 people of Indian origin, third largest group after African and Irish origin people. The Indian community here was different than neighbouring Trinidad or Guyana. There were no big owners of Cocoa or rice plantations. Many had shops or banana plantations.

Like other African island Indians faced the ire of local African commuity, as the unemployment increased after the arrival of the Indians. Plantation owners preferred Indians over the Africans. But gradually Indians assimilated well. Many converted to Christianity and started using local last names. Jamaican Indians chose English over their Bhojpuri language. But many kept celebrating some Hindu festivals like Diwali.

They are the ones who brought mango and tamarind to Jamaica. They even brought mongoose to Jamaica! These mongooses became aggressive in Jamaica, feeding not only on the rats, but even the eggs and hens. In India mongooses rarely climb trees, but in Jamaica they began to do so. A cultural change Indians brought in Jamaica, was by bringing Cannabis.

This addiction spread like wildfire on the island. Whereas Indians were used to it, locals became slow and dull after consuming it. The Rastafarian community loved hemp so much that they made it a part of their life. This community was started by Leonard Percival Howell. He spent his life among Indians at Clarendon. He would sing *Jai Kali Mai* devotional song after smoking hemp. He began to carry hairlocks like ascetics from India, which later became their identity. One of the popular Rastafarian singer Bob Marley flaunted these locks. He even named his son after the cricketer Rohan Kanhai as Rohan Marley. Indian cricketer Sunil Gavaskar also did the same and named his son

Rohan Gavaskar. Famous pop and reggae artist Diana King's mother is of Indian origin.

Some Jamaican Indians became jewellers and made gold bangles which are still popular in Jamaica. Especially Jaadu Singh Ji opened many jewellery shops in Kingston.

Guadeloupe

Since sugar production was decreasing on Reunion Island, France tried to focus on this small Caribbean Island. Unfortunately, an earthquake in 1843 destroyed many sugar mills, but they wished to continue production. 344 Indians were brought here on the ship Loreal on 25 December 1854. In 1864, another lot of 330 labourers were brought from Madras. Till 1884 about 40,000 labourers were brought to this island. After that the agreement between Britain and France ended, because of many complaints about difficult life there. About 10,000 Girmitiya died after coming to this island. Some of the labourers were taken to another nearby island Saint Martin.

This Caribbean Island was different because many Tamil labourers came here, and their descendents live even today. One of them, Henry Sidambram fought for the rights of the labourers and got them French citizenship. Now hardly anyone speaks Tamil here however Indian names can still be found.[7] Some time ago the city Basse-Terre has been made the 'sister city' of Puducherry in India and attempts are being made of recreating ties.

Saint Croix

Saint Croix was the sole Danish colony where *Girmitiya* reached. Denmark had to overcome several hurdles to get this agreement done. It had to give guarantee that labourers would be kept well. Only one ship Mars reached Saint Croix on 13 June 1863 with 321 people. Out of these 3 people died.[8]

As soon as they landed here, just like other islands they were divided into several small groups. Maximum of 64 people were sent to Lower Bethlehem Estate. British government took a hefty sum for the labourers, which was an expensive deal for them. The labourers who came here either went back to India or went to Trinidad. Most probably nobody from those original families lives there now. Although people from other Caribbean Islands settled there later.

Saint Kitts and Nevis

These two islands in the Caribbean were among the last destinations, with 315 labourers in Saint Nevis and 337 labourers in Saint Kitts.

On 3 June 1861 the ship Dartmouth reached Saint Kitts. This information was recorded by Captain Eelis and was kept in the proctor's office at Fort Williams Calcutta. Among the 361 people who had set off, only 332 could make it. 24 people died on the way, and 5 died after reaching there.

Captain Eelis has recorded their origins from: -

Saheb Gangay (Gaya)- 85

Ranchi- 84

Purulia- 40

Hazaribagh- 33

Shahabad (Aara)- 25

Munger- 22

Some people came from Patna, Azimabad and Jalasor too.

Maximum of 29 labourers were sent to Devaar Estate. These people were sent in small groups of 20-25 to various estates, and many families got separated. Some of these labourers refused to work. The names of these protestors are mentioned- Brahmdatt, Dhijan and Shampod.

Surprisingly, within four years, all of them became Christians and adopted Christian names. This quick assimilation wasn't witnessed on any other island. As soon as the contract expired the labourers from here went to Trinidad and Guyana. In 1982, their documents kept in the courthouse got destroyed in a fire. Today only 0.2% of the total population are Indians.

• The same ship sank later in Fiji.

On Nevis Island, the ship Syria landed on 30 March 1874.• About 20% people returned to India after finishing the contract while the rest moved to neighbouring islands. In the Cotton Ground Village of Nevis Island there are a few families of Indian origin, who might have stayed back. I got information about the family of John Clarke whose grandfather Bhagirath and grandmother Mangru had come from India. They too converted to Christianity. Most of the people of this Clarke family are in New York and only one household is there on Nevis Island.[9]

Belize

Belize is a small Central American country, close to Honduras and Panama. Documents suggest that the first group brought here were the prisoners of the 1857 revolt from India. It is a strange coincidence that today on its other shore is the infamous Guantanamo Bay Camp. Thousands of these soldiers were made to do physical labour in Belize, and that village of the rebel Indian soldiers is known as Calcutta.

No information could be found about any ship arriving in Belize, but the agents from Belize went over to Jamaica to pick up labourers. Between 1880 and 1917 about 3400 Indians were brought from Jamaica and sent to sugarcane plantations in Toldos and Corozal. In these districts you can still find Indian faces and Bihari names, but they have assimilated into the local culture.

At present there are about 7,000 people of Indian origin in Belize and Hindi speakers can also be found at some places.[10]

Reference

1. Eric E. Williams, Capitalism and Slavery, University of North Carolina Press, 1944
2. Marina Carter, Voices from Indenture, Experiences of Indians Migrants in the British Empire, Leicester University Press, 1966
3. Gaiutra Bahadur, Coolie Women: The Odyssey of Indenture, Hurst Company, 2013 (Secondary Source)
4. John Bigelow, Jamaica in 1850: Or, the Effects of Sixteen Years of Freedom on a Slave Colony, The University of Michigan, 1851

5. Harinder Singh Sohal, The East Indian Indentureship System in Jamaica 1845-1917, Ph.D. Thesis, University of Waterloo, 1980
6. Walton Look Lai, Indentured Labour, Caribbean Sugar: Chinese and Indian Migrants to the British West Indies, 1838-1918, The Johns Hopkins University Press, Baltimore and London, 1993
7. Christian Schreckenberg, Le'Immigration Indiana en Guadeloupe, 1848-1923, Ph.D. Thesis, University of Provenance
8. Coolie Journal 1863 (Excerpt from the book Indian Indenture in the Danish West Indies written by Lomash Roopnarayan, published by Springer,2016)
9. Martez Hassan Khan and Others, The Legacy of Indian Indenture: Historical and Contemporary aspects of Migration and Diaspora, Routledge, 2016
10. Indo Caribbean Genealogy (Shamsuddin's email), Internet Source
11. Martez Hassan Khan and Others, The Legacy of Indian Indenture, Historical and Contemporary aspects of Migration and Diaspora, Routledge, 2016

Suriname

"Let's go to the country of Siri Ram, we shall find everything there."

"What are you saying? Siri Ram?"

"Yes, Yes, Siri Ram."

"Jai Siri Ram."

Arkati agents named Suriname as Siri Ram, and this was the reason why people huddled into the ships left for Suriname.

Munshi ji's journey

Munshi Rehman Khan was not just an educated Muslim but was also a religious and ideal person. When he watched Hindu *Girmitiyas* throw away their *Janeu* (sacred thread) in the Hooghly River, he felt extremely sad and angry. He wrote that people are morally falling here, becoming degenerate, eating anything, sleeping with anyone. They are losing their Indianness. Munshi ji wrote in his autobiography that on the ship he would recite the Ramayana to the people on the ship. He was a Muslim but was educated enough to read the Ramayana. One of the reasons why he was called Munshi.

Rehman was a Pathan from the Bharkadi village of Hamirpur (United Province). When he reached Suriname in 1889, he was also sent to the plantations like others. In his group there were five men and a lower caste Hindu woman. As per the tradition that Hindu woman was asked to choose her partner and she chose Rehman. He might have been the best in some or other ways among those five men. But Rehman wasn't ready for this impromtu marriage.

Rehman writes that, this was without his wish, and he kept a distance from this woman even after the wedding. But whenever he wanted to run away from her, she would start wailing, "Who would look after me?" When he tried an intervention from the overseer, the woman claimed that she was pregnant with Rehman's baby. The plantation owner ordered that he had to pay the baby's expenses for six months. Although Rehman denied any such possibility, he had to live with her and bear her expenses.

Rehman must have left her after being free from the plantation. In his version of story, Rehman appears to be the victim. But one feels pity for the woman who had to choose someone just for security and create a false pretense of conceiving a baby.

Munshi Rehman has expressed his initial days well in this poem: -

All of us came from India here for a job
Girmit was difficult and then cultivated government land
In the Commissionerate Allahabad, district Hamirpur
Bimbar is my Thana and Bharakadi my village
Achievement and money in the years in motherland
On the 13th of the enemy month, to Dutch Guyana I came
Spent five years of Girmitya life at Kothi Rustamlast
Then as Sardar for 20 years under Manager Hurst.

For his Bundeli and Hindi writing he is considered the first Hindi poet of Suriname.[3]

Revolution of Kate Kollock

Were there Indian officers on the ship? How nice it would have been if this was so? In this search I found about a ship that arrived in Suriname in 1874. When I was collecting information about this ship, I came to know that the surgeon superintendent of this ship was Dr. Bipin Bihari Dutt. He had studied medicine from Edinburgh (Scotland.) But he was the only Indian officer on just one ship, which I could find in records. This seemed surprising to me. The issue with Suriname is also that all documents and books are in Dutch, and it was difficult for me to translate these. But this information linked back to a crucial fact hence I kept on searching.

Did Dr. Dutt grew compassionate towards these *Girmitiya*? Did one Indian stand to protect other Indians in the face of discrimination? He not only helped them but encouraged them for a revolt.

There was some issue between a white officer and two women on the ship. Dr. Dutt was sad about the oppression of the labourers and was protesting this. Gradually this protest got organized. Soon ensued a war between the sailors and the *Girmitiyas*. Sailors were attacking them, throwing bones on them. Dr. Dutt was at the root of this revolt who had asked the *Girmitiyas* not to obey the officers.

A rumor spread among the Girmitiyas that as soon as they would reach Suriname their throats would be slit, and they would be thrown in the sea. This further fueled the revolt.

Somehow this revolt stopped, and the ship reached Suriname. Dr. Dutt was chargesheeted and was strangely accused of distributing liquor among sailors and *Girmitiyas*. Doctors giving some Brandy to sick *Girmitiyas* wasn't anything new and even if Dr. Dutt gave them, it was not a big mistake. Dr. Dutt was banished from the ship along with his family on an island midway (St. Helena?) and sent back to London. Never again an Indian officer was employed on the ship.

In some weird way, this ship was cursed. In 1878 this ship sank in the sea on a voyage from San Francisco.[4-5]

Baba and Mai

Suriname is a small country in the Northern tip of South America. It was initially a British colony in the sixteenth century. In 1667, the Dutch (Netherlands) occupied it and began to produce coffee and sugar. Many slaves were kept ranging from the natives Arawak Indians to the African slaves. In 1795 the French got control of it for a short while. In 1813 after Napoleon's defeat, the king of Netherlands William I occupied it again. Definitely because of the wealth of this land, various powers kept exchanging it among them. In 1863 slavery was abolished in Dutch colonies including Suriname.

After abolition of slavery, some Dutch farmers were brought from the city of Groningen, but half of them died. Then some Chinese workers were brought from Indonesia who ran away after the completion of five years of contract. Nobody was ready to settle in Suriname. Some old African slaves were kept on ten years contract, who too didn't continue in farms. Now there was only one option- India!

British sold Indian workers to a Dutch colony. Calcutta already had the embassy of Netherlands, so this business was convenient. Dutch took some time to understand the *Arkati* agents and initially the agents took advantage of them. Between 1873 and 1888, if a labourer eloped from the depot, refused to travel, deemed unfit or die, the agent would still get his full payment. Later this rule was abolished, as it Dutch suffered economic loss. They began to give sixty percent advance to the *Arkati* to catch the labourer and bring them. The costs of their travel and food was covered. Once they were permanently employed, the rest of 40% was paid.[6] This wasn't a bad deal either. *Arkati* preferred to come to the Dutch as they bribed with some extra money to fill their ships first.[7] Workers initially brought for Demerara would be sent to Suriname. For Indians, it made no difference whether it was Demerara or Suriname!

The first Suriname agent at Calcutta was William Durham, but the officials of Suriname had various complaints against him. He did not send workers properly. He was also accused that it his wife and daughter were doing his job. At last, he was removed, and a Dutch man Van Custom was made the agent.[8] He did a lot of work for better management on the ship and the camp for Suriname (Kampong).

Indentured labour to Suriname can't be strictly called 'new slavery' because most had come here of their free will. By the time immigration started for Suriname many ships had already gone to Mauritius and Fiji. They were aware of the pros and cons. Although many people complained that they were beguiled (*bharmaay dihis*).[9]

On 5th May 1873 the first ship *Lallarookh* reached the capital city Paramaribo in Suriname. When Indians were getting off the ship the old creole African slaves shouted - *Jobo Tanbasi*! This meant that the Whites are still the king. One slavery ended and other has begun.

Their landing place place was called Coolie Depot and now stands two statues of a man and woman there called 'Baba and Mai'. The immigration day is celebrated here on 5th June.

On the *Lallarookh* ship there were 296 Braj, 75 Avadhi, 49 Bhojpuri and Magahi, 14 Bengali, 2 Marathi and Gujarati, 1 Oriya, 1 Rajasthani, 1 Punjabi, 1 Chhattisgarhi and 5 from other unknown regions.[10] These had people from all castes and both Hindus and Muslim religions. There were more people from lower castes but there were some from the Brahmin and the Kshatriya caste too. Brahmins discarded their sacred thread in the Hooghly and said –

"Hey Mother Ganges! We offer you our religion and our traditions. We are going to the foreign lands becoming Shudras. If we come back, we shall wear it again or *Jai Harihar*!"

It seemed that Dutch were less cruel than British. Their ships had better arrangements, with a European doctor and an interpreter. Every day 500 liters of clean water was provided. Besides this the workers' rooms had arrangements for fresh air. The death rate of workers was 7 per thousand, much lesser than the rest of the ships.

In this context the mention of Agent general Roosevelt is a must, he was so kind that as soon as the *Girmitiya* children came off the ship, he would lift them up in his arms. In those times Whites picking up the Coolie children was rare and exceptional. He was called 'Coolie Papa'. When anyone had an issue, they would come to his house in Paramaribo and present their complaint. Another Dr. Romain is mentioned who was often on the ships and spoke good Hindi.[11]

In Suriname the workers were categorized differently- able bodied and disable bodied. Able bodied were healthy adult men whose daily wage was 60 cents. Disable bodied were weak adults, women, and teenagers between ten to sixteen years of age who were given forty cents daily.[12] After this categorization, workers were sent to different plantations.

The biggest sugar company of Suriname was *Nederlandse Handelmaatschappij* (NHM) whose biggest plantation was in Marienburg. Indians began to increase their dominance in all plantations whereas that of former African slaves began to diminish. In

1873 there were about 15,000 Creole workers and by 1913 there were only 500 Creoles left. Creole people were trouble for the owners as they didn't work properly and were aggressive. Indians were obedient and hardworking.[13]

Punishments given in Suriname were as per the Dutch law and weren't as severe as on other islands. Many workers wanted to go to jail so that they could rest there! Although, there are mentions of prison breaks and running away from plantations. According to a report in the *Girmitiya* period in Suriname a total of 227 people had run away.• Once some workers ran away into the jungles near Marienburg, with stolen hens and began farming corn there. When the officers caught them, they were surprised to see so many arrangements there.

Although Indians were in the Dutch colony of Suriname, they were the citizens of British India. Thus, they weren't strictly under Dutch jurisdiction and protested with relative immunity. In 1897, many Dutch women protested by by lying on the train tracks. In 1899 labourers put sugarcane fields on fire in Marienburg. But some revolts ended in a gruesome manner.[14]

Zorg en Hoop revolt, 1884

Zorg en Hoop was a Scottish plantation in Suriname, where about 400 workers were employed. People here were oppressed by an overseer Knot who made them work more and the wages weren't fair in comparison. One day when the oppression seemed to have crossed its limits, four Indian labourers beat him up. The commissioner reached the plantation to punish them. But by then the revolt had become fierce. About a hundred Indians were waiting with axes and sticks. They were being led by a man named Ramjani and a woman named Jani Tetary. Ramjani was a Hindu and Jani Tetary a Muslim.

Seeing their anger, the commissioner returned that day but returned to the Coolie Lines two days later with 50 soldiers. The army

• In Suriname, Kantraki term is preferred over Girmitiyas. Kantraki origins from Contract (Dutch- Kantrak).

men were trying to scare them by beating drums whereas the labourers were shouting, "*Aawa, himmat hai toh aawa*" (Come! if you have the courage, come!)

Jani Tetary belonged to Maner in Patna (Bihar) and came to Suriname in1880 with her ten years old child. Later she also adopted a Hindu child. She was a courageous woman whom all admired. Travelling solo as a Muslim woman so far on a ship speaks volumes about her courage.

Janey Tetary (Courtesy- Moti and Pavan Marhe)

In her leadership women collected stones, bottles, and lumps of mud. As soon as the army moved in, they began to attack. Tetary was shot with a bullet on her back and died. Six other Indians were martyred along with her. Ramjani tried to kill himself by jumping into the river but was caught. After this revolt the famous 'Coolie Papa' Roosevelt came in to pacify the Indians.[15]

Some years back, the statue of an English General Leon was removed in Paramaribo and replaced by a statue of Jani Tetary•. The statue of a Girmitiya woman, replacing a white man's statue has its own symbolic value.

• Ironically, the statue of the English General Leon was also put by an Indian Sheetal Prasad because of their cordial relations.

Moharram Revolt, 1891

Moharram is an important festival of the Muslims also known as Husseini. On this day the *Girmitiya* of all religions would take out the Tazia procession with all weapons and arms. Conflicts happened on the issue that who would first immerse the Tazia first in water. This was also the day when the *Girmitiya* took out their angst. In 1891, things got heated up.

There was conflict regarding the processions in Geertruidenberg, Jolene and Marienburg. When the officials came to intervene, they all got together and put up a fight with them. Some of them were caught and taken to the court. People started pelting stones at the Attorney General office. When police tried to push them with rifle butts, they began to hurl stones on them. At last, police started firing and five *Girmitiya* were killed.

After this firing many *Girmitiya* ran away and his in the jungles with their families, but they were later convinced to return.[16] Again Coolie Papa Roosevelt pacified the workers, but he died after a few days. Several Indians took part in his death procession.

Next month the revenge of this firing was taken by a worker named Sheikh Abdul, who killed the plantation owner Jaglust. Sheikh Abdul was given the death sentence.

Marienburg Massacre, 1902

Since 1873 about ten revolts had happened in Suriname, out of which this was the biggest. It was the month of July; the workers went on strike on the issue of wages. Dutch income from sugarcane was decreasing and hence the wages of the workers were also being decreased. Complaints from the plantation Manager Mavor was mounting. The British supervisor Windhem wrote that Chumru, Matabadal and Abdul were beaten with iron rods. Revolt was bound to happen.

Mavor came riding a horse and ensured some increase in wages. But the labourers didn't agree and said that they wanted to meet the collector. Three labourers were given the pass to meet the collector. But as soon as Mavor was about to return, the labourers attacked him with sugarcane sticks. Mavor raced away on his horse while his overseer took the train. A crowd of two hundred people was chasing them shouting, "Kill him! Kill him!" When they tried to call the police, the labourers cut off the phone wires and uprooted the poles. Finally, they caught Mavor and killed him.

Hearing about this incident, the collector came with 121 soldiers and arrested a few people. This agitated the labourers even more and they gathered at the bridge between the office and the factory. The labourers waiting on this bridge were randomly fired at and 24 *Girmitiyas* were killed. There bodies were buried without any identification. They all died nameless.[17] A memorial has been built for these Girmitiyas in 2006. Indian Foreign Ministry was also sent the name of these deceased and the names of their villages. In 2012, Archaeologist Benjamin Mitrasingh got the permission to find and exhume their graves.

Moti Marhe in Marienburg estate (courtesy- Moti Marhe)

In 1902 there was another revolt under the leadership of Jhumpa Raiguru, in Alliance plantation.[18] Another Indian soldier *Girmitiya* Jatan was accused of organised rebellion and several sticks were found in a field in Paramaribo, but this revolt never happened. Revolts happened more on sugarcane plantations and less on coffee or cocoa plantations, which suggests that life was tougher on sugarcane plantations.

The writer of this Surinami-Bhojpuri song is unknown, but it describes their story well-

Dreaming on board the Lalrukhwa ship
All of us came together to Suriname as Contraki
When from the depot in Calcutta we boarded the ship
Heard a lot about farming and hard work
We listened and remained quiet
Passing many countries
Together we made homes here and spend our lives here
You live and I live, our country now Suriname re!

Women of Suriname

"Is the oldie home?"

A popular saying in Suriname•

Compared to other islands the proportion of women remained better in Suriname. The Dutch government wrote clearly in their agreement with the British government that they required a female/male ratio of 40/60. But this just remained on paper. It was difficult for *Arkati* agents to maintain this proportion. They tried to convince the officials in Suriname that Indian women who wanted to leave India were most probably sex workers and would bring deadly diseases. Many widows also felt suffocated in their homes after their husbands' death and wanted to leave. But widows and sex workers were not liked much by plantation owners. They felt that these women would work less and try to seduce the men.[19]

• From a conversation with Prof. Chan Choenni as he puts it – *Budhwa Hai Ghare?*

The question is whether immigration was a vehicle for women emancipation? Matai Chattarpalli who had come in 1898 on board the ship *Avon* was separated from her husband. In 1904 when she was free,

Janaki, a Sarnami woman (courtesy- Moti Marhe)

she didn't even try to find out about what happened to her husband. It is possible that she might be in a relation with someone else or wanted to get rid of the relationship imposed on her in India.

Looking at the pictures of Surinami women, one can see that tall, well-built fair men were married to petite, dark women. Women had many ornaments and smoked marijuana. Some women had more than one husband. Some would marry older men because they had more money. Hence the saying, "Is the oldie home?"

They lived mostly on their own terms. Although they did inculcate the seeds of Indian culture in their own daughters and were strict with them. Especially after 1920 there was a 'honourable' women campaign and in which girls had to protect their 'honour' relations with other men or pre-marital relationships were prohibited.

Some reports of women being sexually and domestically exploited are mentioned. Especially setting a woman named Jasoda on fire is described.[20] In 1907 on a ship an officer named Arnold Balmer raped a small girl of about seven-eight years named Saroda, and then sent her back with some biscuits. Saroda had come on the ship with her father and like any other curious kid roam, would about on the ship. Such kids were easy prey, especially if mother was not with them and they had to sleep with stranger women away from the father. Despite Saroda's complaint and statement on the ship nothing was done against Balmer. Even her father didn't pay much heed to this. There is another strange incident too. A woman was first sent to sleep with another man by her own husband in lieu of some loan. But when she returned, he slit both her hands due to guilt and anger.[21]

After Girmitiya Period

Between 1873 and 1916, a total of 34,000 labourers were brought from India. Many among these decided to return to India after completing their contract but about 23, 000 stayed back and decided to settle here. In 1910 under the leadership of Pandit Sheetal Prasad Dubey, an immigration association named *Surinaamsche Immigranten Vereniging* was established. Sheetal Prasad was a sharp man. His widowed mother had come to Suriname with him after the death of her husband. His mother had never done farming and had found a job as a nurse in the hospital. Thus, Sheetal Prasad grew up differently from other *Girmitiyas*, got better education, bought his own home in Paramaribo, and became an elite urban man. He was like a god to the labourers and would sit on a chair, while labourers would come to him with complaints. He was called Sheetal Maharaj. He was the main interpreter for the Dutch and often accompanied *Girmitiyas* on the ship. His work also included positive marketing in India to get labourers. This is probably the only example where an Indian *Girmitiya* technically transforming into an agent. He was in fact an adopted son of Agent General Lyon.

Sheetal Dubey was sent to all sub-depots in 1913 to assure people that the condition of workers in Suriname was good. Due to his efforts, they received the last lot consisting of 45 people. In 1920 Sheetal Prasad even went to meet Indian leaders like Madan Mohan Malviya. He argued that if this tradition was stopped, then Sarnami Indians would become weak. If there are more Indians, dominance could be maintained.[22] His fears were not entirely ungrounded.

When Indian indenture stopped, about 33,000 people were called from Indonesia. I was curious as to why they didn't get workers from Dutch Indonesia before. Were Indian labourers cheaper? Or better?

According to the Census in 2012 there were 1,48,443 citizens of Indian origin in Suriname. The Dutch people of Netherlands called them 'Hindoestanen'. Many people call them *Kalkatiya* because most came via Calcutta. Most of the Indians who stayed back in Suriname took to farming. This was more convenient after 1895 when they were given some land after their contract was over. Those who stayed back were also given a sum of a hundred guilder. Gradually the sugar trade depleted, and sugarcane fields also decreased. As compared to 80 plantations in 1863 there were only 4 left in 1940.

Indians began to plant rice. In the North-west area of Suriname, Nickerie, there were many Indian fields. They kept buying more land and became entrepreneurial farmers. By 1940, 90% of farming was in the hand of Indians. During the first world war, the Indians in Suriname grew a lot of rice and exported.

Surinami Indians also made their own village panchayat and chose their village leader. If someone troubled a woman or did some other bad deed, he was labelled outcaste and thrown out of the village. Later he would pay a fine and return. Due to the lack of women, there were many old bachelors who were known as *Mughalisiya*. They would look after the kids of the family like uncles and other village affairs.

Despite economic prosperity, the social reputation and political strength of Indians was still lesser than the Whites and Africans. During the Second World War, Suriname came under the German attack and their big ship *Gaasler* docked in Paramaribo. Natives and probably some Indians attacked at them. The captain had to sink their own ship. Some remains of the ship can still be found there.

The social condition of Indians began to improve after the Second World War. Their children began to go to schools and gradually an intellectual class of Indians was created who were at par with the Whites and the Africans. Now they began leaving their villages to come to the cities. By 1964 about 32% population in Paramaribo consisted of Indians. A large proportion of those coming to cities were Muslims. Hindus were still in villages mostly.[23]

One of the famous banks today ABN(AMRO) was established by the blood and sweat of these Indian *Girmitiyas*. It had started from the sugar company NHM that I have previously mentioned. This NHM along with Deutsche bank became ABN in 1964. The same year one of its units became the AMRO bank. These are now big banks of Netherlands and Suriname with branches in India as well. After discovery of Bauxite mines, Suriname became one of the rich countries in the world.

Religion in Suriname

In Suriname 70% of Indians are Hindus and the rest are Muslims or converted to Christianity. This is also distinctive about Suriname that it initially had many relations between Hindus and Muslims. The Indians coming from the culture of *parivar banabe* (making a family) tried to make their families irrespective of the caste or religion. There are many Surinami families that have Hindus, Muslims, and Christians under one roof.

Although some traces of casteism remained initially, like Brahmins initiated rituals and tried to do religious propaganda. They were given the titles of Maharaja and Maharajin. But only 5% were Brahmins and 12% were Kshatriya. There was a community of untouchables categorised as Chamars. When one of them returned to India with lot of money, they were beaten by the upper caste people. He returned to Suriname and today his family is one of the richest and most intellectual families of Suriname. This one example makes it clear that how being free from the oppression of caste led to the progress of the untouchables.[24]

Arya Samaj came to Suriname in 1912 and tried to oppose the dominance of the Brahmins by insisting on the reading of the Vedas. Munshi Rehman writes that the Arya Samaji's re-planted the seeds of caste in a society that had become casteless. In 1929 the Brahmins got formally established and weighed better socially as compared to the Arya Samaj followers.[25]

In Islam there weren't any Sunni-Shia conflicts, but Ahmadiyyas began to grow and now about 30% Muslims are Ahmadiyya. Indonesian muslims stayed away from Indian Muslims. Their mosques were also different. The direction of the mosques of the Indians was towards the East whereas Indonesian Muslims' mosques were towards the West.[26]

However, later the attention towards religion decreased and Western Culture began to dominate. Munshi Rehman writes:[27]

"Not learning from the scriptures, they learn adverse things from evil people
Given up all religious conduct they behave as if they are European
Shaving off their moustaches and beards they try to look like a Christian
By paying the hairdresser a rupee and a half, try weird hairstyles in vain
Where the black woman performs her drama, you dance with her in

costume
Drink alcohol and party and sing the Black tones along
Leaving the married wives at home you keep the black women as concubines"

Still just like Mauritius and Fiji, people in Suriname were able to retain their Indian culture largely. During Diwali, the world's largest Diya is lit at the Independence Square in Paramaribo. Indians in Suriname were multi-lingual. They spoke Surinami-Bhojpuri, Urdu, Dutch and African Creole language Sranan Tongo as well. Sarnami was taught in some schools there and many people speak it. In 1924, under the leadership of lawyer C. R. Biswamitra an organisation named Nav Yug Uday was founded which worked for the spread of Hindi. Since 1983, a magazine titled Bhasha was published in Hindi/Surinami from Paramribo. Suriname has Hindi newspapers and Surinami Radio channels.

'Mahashay' Sukhdev Choenni. His father Halkhori Sahu migratedrom Anathpur, Bihar to Suriname in 1889 (Courtesy-Chan Choenni)

Like the Chutney music of the Caribbean the *Baithak Gaana* from here is famous. One of the ministers Ashwin Adhin himself plays the table very well. The Laxmi Samaj here organises festivals of classical music.

Why did culture retain itself in Suriname but perished in nearby islands like Guyana and Jamaica? Professor Chan Choenni answers this question. When Indians came here the language was Dutch, whereas on other islands it was English. Dutch wished them to preserve their *aadat* (habits), in a way to keep them as agrarian society, and not rise in the rungs of power. Thus, they kept speaking their language, and preserving their culture, while missing the political power to some extent. But the conditions changed, and they gradually realised the importance of learning Dutch and English for their betterment.

Indians in Politics

When India got independence, it energized the Indians in Suriname too. A song sung at that time explains the situation well: -

"The country has become free, let's stay together
Don't create trouble in this country
Whether you live in Suriname or return to India
Don't become Christian in this country
Since there has been trouble, Hindu- Muslim are together
All have been ruined together in this country
Obey what Gandhiji says, don't follow your own wish
Now you won't find a destination in this country
Listen both Hindus and Muslims, be known as India's sons
Do not fight in this country."[28]

Indians were not out of politics. In fact, the largest political party there VHP (*Vooruitstrevende Hervormingspartij)* was Indian. Second largest party NPK was of the Africans. For many years there was a political alliance between Indian leader named Lacchman and Creole leader Pengel. But after Pengel's death in 1970 things began to change. New Creole leader Aaron raised the Creole front 'Cricomacca' which was anti-Indian. Indians were dismissed from high posts and there was some arson too which instilled fear in the heart of Indians.

In 1975 when Suriname became independent, many Indians thought that Suriname won't be able to stay free and the economy would collapse. They also felt that they would be discriminated against, and girls would be raped. In 1980 there was a coup led by a military under Bouterse and many political rivals were killed. Then cycles of democracy and coup continued. In 1982, one Indian Ram Dutt Misra was also the Prime Minister for some time. Bouterse returned to power after spending many years in prison. In 2017 there has been an INTERPOL warrant against President Bouterse regarding drug trade (Cocaine.) But since he was the President, he couldn't be arrested. In 2020, Chan Santokhi, a *Girmitiya* descendent became the president.

Netherlands

We work during the day, and see dreams at night
Aja's face looks like somewhat mine
The name of our ship was Lalla Rookhwa
The name of our country now Netherlands Babua
Flying KLM, we left Surinamwa
When I remember you, I look for history
Unlike Panchamrit, the essence of this story
The ache of this tale pierces my heart
Why did they leave India, I can't get that!

- Jit Narain, Surinami, poet of Netherland[29]

Looking for a father

When I was writing this book, I tried to contact many people to learn about the *Girmitiyas*. I never received any reply from many contacts. Some said that they could not help as they have no links with the *Girmitiyas* now. And some people became very emotional. They had so many questions, but I had few answers. I only know what can be found from the archives. Maybe by reading this book some reader might find their lost extended family in India. There are many people who have one piece of a paper and are looking for the other piece. In this journey a letter was found that reached me from Amsterdam via Delhi.

Village- Vaina, District- Rajpur, Thana- Sikandra, Kanpur rural, 1914

20 yr old Parsadi Ram Sahay reached Kanpur sub-depot with his wife Durga Ramju and their two sons. This was the time when the *Girmitiya* tradition was in its last leg. There was massive negative publicity against it in all the villages. Yet, Parsadi chose to travel to Suriname from a Thakur (Rajput) -dominated village in Western Uttar Pradesh.

The ship *SS Indus IV* set sail from Calcutta on its last voyage•. Prasadi's family reached Suriname after a forty-day long sea voyage. He was among those few fortunate people who was taking along his family with him. When Parsadi reached Suriname, he and his family were sent to a plantation where they spent five years of the contract. In Suriname they had another child. Unfortunately, wife contracted Spanish flu like fever and died. Parsadi, now a father of three children, became alone, but he completed his contract.

Parsadi's life story becomes a mystery thereon. In 1920 he left his children behind in an orphanage in Suriname and returned to India. He had become depressed and lonely after the demise of his wife. He left the children behind because he thought that the lives of children would be better in Suriname. His children kept waiting for him, but he never returned.

When Suriname became free, many families migrated to Netherlands, including Prasadi's eldest son, now a young man. How an orphan made it so far is unimaginable!

Decades later, in 1999 he travelled to Vaini village in search of his father and extended family. He took the same journey from Calcutta that his father Parsadi might have taken. He left with his father at age of 6 years, and now he was 91 yrs old. The India of his faint childhood memories had completely changed now. It was now a free country basking in the IT boom.

When he finally reached his village and touched its soil, he began rolling in it like a toddler. He wondered why his parents had left this golden land and settled so far away? What did they get?

• When the ship that took Prasadi returned to India, the same year a German ship looted and sank it.

In the village nobody could tell anything about Parsadi. Maybe he never returned to his village. Did he take up a job in Calcutta? Did he remarry? At the time he returned to India in 1920, *Girmitiya* ships had almost stopped plying. The *Sutlej*, that set sail for Fiji in 1916 is considered as the last *Girmitiya* ship to have sailed. So, it seems impossible for him to return from India. In 1921 the last Surinami contract from India had ended.

Hughes Tinker writes about the condition of Calcutta in 1920-[30]

"These *Girmitiya* who had returned to India, spent their saved wealth in the village, and returned to Calcutta to go back on the next ship. But there were no depots here anymore. The place that was Surinami Depot was made *Apravasi Mitr Sehyog Samiti*/Immigrant Friends Cooperative Society now, where they would get shelter. Coolie and *Girmitiya* period were over. The India that had advocated the abolition of this tradition, now had no place for them. Sugarcane fields in distant lands where they were troubled so much, now seemed like their only hope. This was a strange end of a strange story."

Parsadi's son left behind his visiting card to the villagers and returned to Amsterdam. Two years later when he received a call from Dhirendra Pal Singh from his village, he was elated. Maybe Dhirendra Pal Singh had some news of his father. Parsadi's son invited him to Amsterdam and when he met him, he cried like a child. He hoped that his father had remarried and had children and that his half-siblings were still somewhere in India. His eyes got moist thinking about this.[31]

Sarnami Indians

June 1943

When the Sikh Brigade of the Azad Hind Fauj (Indian National Army) reached Netherlands, the country was occupied by Germany. Subhash Chandra Bose met Hitler and asked for help to tackle the British Army in India, and his army underwent training in Dresden. There is no definite number known but it is estimated that about 3000 soldiers were trained. Today there are many Sikhs in Netherlands, but most have come in the 1970s. Did any Sikh stay behind from this army?

1975 Sarnami Indians

Indians had been coming from Suriname to Netherlands for education and jobs. Having Dutch citizenship, they could easily travel to Netherlands. When Suriname got its independence in 1975 many of them ran away from there and settled here. They are known as Sarnami, and in 2017, there were about 2,90,000 Sarnami Indians residing here. Most of them live in Hague. When Idi Amin ordered the expulsion of Asians, a huge group of people of Indian origin came from Uganda. As Sarnami Indians came here in large numbers they created a small India here. Till this date they remain connected to each other. Many have married amongst themselves. They still speak Sarinami-Bhojpuri language, but the new generation is not so keen on learning or speaking Bhojpuri. After Bollywood has become popular here, Hindi is also spoken and understood by many. Most of them however speak only Dutch.

Sarnamis also celebrate various Indian festivals. All the homes that I visited had Indian item. Many houses even have harmonium and sitar. They often come to India but hey rarely visit their ancestral village. Rather, they go to Mumbai, Delhi, Kolkata, or Goa as a tourist. But they do feel a sense of belongingness with Indians. When they visit India, they say that everything here reminds them of Suriname, be it — the fields, the shops and the people. As if Suriname is a part of India only.

Raj Mohan is a popular Sarinami Bhojpuri ghazal and pop singer in Netherlands. He often comes to India and visits the village of his ancestors. One person, who is now from a well to do family in Netherlands, only knew that his paternal grandfather used to talk about a big banyan tree in his village. He was fortunate to find that tree and his extended family. But not all are so fortunate.

Sarnami Bhojpuri

I was very surprised when I laid my hands on the book *Suru se Suru kar*. Alexander had written this book in 1975 in Dutch Roman script to teach children Sarinami grammar. Bhojpuri language and grammar has been explained so well along with pictures. Many Dutch words have been incorporated. Moti Marhe researched in Suriname, India and Netherlands and wrote an exceptional book on Sarnami grammar. He also suggests that we must use Sarnam instead of Suriname. Sarinami is a mix of Bhojpuri and Avadhi and is spoken by Sarnami Indians. Although now the script is Roman or Dutch!

For instance, read this Sarnami New Testament-

"Parmeswar pahiele aapan sanesian pathaaike apane ke Israel ke djaatie khaatien djanaais hai. Oesabke tjaahat raha sab koi se bataawe ke aur aapan tjaal-tjalan se dekhaawe ke kie oe kaisan hai. Pahiela djabaana me oe aapan sanesian se koetjh poestak liekhwaais. Ie sab liekhal baat ek me okar pahiela poestak hai. Tab oe aapan Beta Jiesoe ke doenia me pathaais. Oe Parmeswar hai aur bhie iensaan hoi gail hai. Oe manai log ke sab baat siekhaais djaun okar Pieta ose bolies raha. Ekare baad Parmeswar koetjh manai log se auro poestak aur tjietthie liekhwaais. Oesab liekhies kie Jiesoe ka bolies aur karies hai, tab ose ka bhail hai aur ekar matlab ka hai. Ie sab liekhal baat Parmeswar ke naawa poestak bolaawal dja hai."[32]

[God first sent his messenger to tell them about his place in Israel. He wished to explain about his looks and behaviour. In those days, messengers were supposed to write a book. The same book is the old book. Then he sent his son Jesus in this world. He is a god, who has become human. He explained to the common people what his father taught to him. Then god made other people write different books. They wrote what Jesus says, what he does and what he means. Those things are called new book of good. (*Translation by author*)

The emergence of Sarinami as a language and books being written in this language is an aspect that must be pondered upon. Just like Fiji Hindi, Sarnami is also an extension of Hindustani language, and its literature can be compared with any regional literature in India. The credit for this goes to the Sarnami people settled in Netherlands. In 1977, Jit Narain's poems were published in Sarinami and Dutch. Later he also started a magazine called *Sarnami*. Before him, Martin Hari Dutt Lacchman Srinivasi had written poems in Sarnami and I have already mentioned about Munshi Rehman in the previous chapter. In 1884

Robin Baldev Singh wrote a novella titled *Isteefa.*What is remarkable about these books was that these are written in the Roman script, and in 1984 with help from the Education department of Netherlands, a standard for Sarinami language was developed in this script.[33]

Reference

1. Munshi Rehman Khan, Jeevan Prakash, Paramaribo (Suriname), 1943
2. Gaiutra Bahadur, Coolie Women: The Odyssey of Indenture, Hurst Company, 2013 (Secondary Source)
3. Sonya Boon, Mutiny? Saltwater stories, Internet source
4. Rajinder Bhagwanbali, 1996. Contracten voor Suriname: Arbeidsmigratie vanuit British-Indie onder het indentured-labourstelsel, 1873–1916.Amrit, 1996
5. Rake Report of Ship, Kate Kellock, 1878, Internet Source
6. R. Bhagwanbali, Ref.4
7. Same Ref. 4
8. Same Ref. 4
9. Interview with Professor Chan Choenni at his residence
10. CJMD Clarke, De Immagratia Dar Hidustanen en Suriname, Amstredam, 1951
11. Interview with Professor Chan Choenni at his residence
12. R. Bhagwanbali, Ref.4
13. Eric Rusken, Caught Between Christianisation, Assimilation and Religious Independency, The Hindustani community in Suriname, Master's Thesis, Faculteit het historische en constitutioneshapen
14. Rosemareen Hofte, Control and Resistance: Indentured labour in Suriname, New West Indian Guide 61 (1-2) 1987, page 1-22
15. Rajinder Bhagwanbali, Tetary - de koppige: het verzet van hindoestanen tegen het Indentured Labour System in Suriname, 1873-1916, Uitgeverij Amrit/Amrit Publishers, 2011
16. Rosemareen Ref. 14
17. Same Ref. 14
18. Interviews of Professor Chan Choenni and Moti Maday in their homes
19. Hughes Tinker, New System of Slavery, The Export of Indian labour overseas, 1830-1920, Oxford University Press, London, 1974
20. Sonya Boon, On Women bodies, violence, economics and escape, Saltwater Stories, Internet source
21. Gaiutra Ref. 2
22. Marteez S. Hassankhan, From Bharatwasi to Hindustani, The end of Indian Indenture and Its Impact on Indians in Suriname, Unpublished
23. Rusken Ref. 13
24. Interview with Professor Chandrasekhar Choenni
25. Munshi Rehman Ref. 1
26. Rusken Ref.13
27. Usharbuddh Arya, Ritual Songs and Folk Songs of Hindus in Suriname, Leiden, 1969

28. Chan Cheonni, Ethnicity and Politics: Political Adaptation of Indians in Suriname, Sociological Bulletin, 63 (3), 2014
29. Kavita Kosh (Internet Source)
30. Hughes Tinker, *New System of Slavery, The Export of Indian Labour Overseas,* 1830-1920, Oxford University Press, London, 1974
31. Telephonic conversations and communication via letters with Dhirendra Pal ji. Rai Ram Sahay's interview in Amsterdam
32. Parmeshwar ke Nawa Pustak, International Bible Society,1997
33. Richard Keith Barz, Jeff Siegel, *Language Transplanted: The Development of Overseas Hindi, Vol. 1.* Modern South Asian Studies Discovery Series, Harrassowitz, 1988

Africa (Zanzibar)

"Nobody is allowed to enter except a Bhatia."

- A board outside the house of a Bhatia in Zanzibar, which Mohandas Karamchand Gandhi refused to enter as per some legend.

From Farrukh to Freddie

The seventies song "We will, we will rock you" by music band Queens is still widely popular. The lead vocalist of this group Freddie Mercury was once and Indian named Farrukh Bulsara. His father Bomi was employed in the British colony of Zanzibar, who continued to stay there after India's independence. An African nanny took care of Farrukh. He was sent to study in a boarding school named St. Peters in Bombay but was later called back to Zanzibar. After 1963 when Zanzibar gained independence, Africans began violent attacks on Indians, and Farrukh's family fled to London.

In London, Farrukh changed his name to Freddie Mercury turning into a sensational singer who died due to AIDS complications. Indian history in Zanzibar may have many such Farrukhs.[1]

How did Indians come to Zanzibar?

The Sultans of Zanzibar kept inviting workers from India for long time. When Sultan Sayyid Barghash came to know that Indian traders were coming to Zanzibar leaving their wives behind he urged the Hindus to bring their wives. Unfortunately, many people still go for work to Africa or Arabian countries leaving their wives and families behind in India as if they are living in nineteenth century. The Sultan sent his personal ship to welcome the first Hindu woman to Zanzibar and gifted her with two hundred and fifty guineas. Later, he opened the doors of old Zanzibar fort for Hindu wome, with silver-coated water taps!

What was the name of the first Hindu woman who came on Sultan's ship to Zanzibar in 1880? This question remains unanswered to me. When I went in search of the the answer, I came to know that four decades before him during Sultan Sayyid's reign, there was his chief custom collector Bhatia Jairam Sevji. He recruited many Bhatias from India, who served as officials and moneylenders.[2] For some reasons, these Bhatias were expelled by Sultan Bargash and gradually their dominance reduced.

Bhatias weren't *Girmitiyas* but business class of Kutch (Gujarat, India). They were vegetarian people always clad in *dhoti*, *janeu* (sacred thread), *kurta* and *topi*. Despite top administrative posts, they too left their wives in India. They earned money in Africa and brought it to India. According to historian Sir Richard Burton, they had intimate relationships with local Arab and native African women.[3]

Thus, all Indians who went across the seas in British India weren't labourers from the lower class but also successful entrepreneur traders, and their history too has been buried with time.

South Africa

"The Coolies are Here"
Headline of the newspaper Natal Mercury•

Free Maria

President D. Clarke of Africa writes in his autobiography that among his ancestors was one Diana from Bengal.[4] How did she come to Africa and when, isn't known. Before I began writing this chapter, I decided to resolve the Diana mystery and I was successful to some extent.

1875, Cape of Good Hope, South Africa

A girl was kidnapped from some obscure village in Bengal and brought to Chittagong. We don't know if she was a Brahmin or a lower caste, a hindu or a muslim. She was taken to Musalipatnam in South India. From there, a Dutch ship set forth for Batavia (Indonesia). I imagine her watching the waves and spread her arms like an eagle on the deck of ship. She had no idea how far she had come.

Some time later, another ship took her from Batavia across the mighty waves of Indian ocean. She probably sat crouched in a corner of her out of fright. Finally, the ship reached the southern-most tip of Africa, Cape of Good Hope.

When she got off the ship, she was made to stand with the other girls of her age. A well-built German soldier Hans Traust became her highest bidder. He brought her home and after a few days took her to church to gave her a name- Maria. Maria remained Traust's slave for ten years. He taught her German, and she forgot to speak

• "The Coolie Here", Natal Mercury, 22 November, 1860

Bengali. Traust was so happy with Maria that he freed her. Maria probably didn't even know that she had been a slave so long.

Maria might have married later, and her genes may be floating somewhere in Africa.[5]

Gurdeen Bhagoo and Mohandas Gandhi

Gurdeen was sent like an ordinary *Ahir* labourer at the age of sixteen from some village near Lucknow to the French Caribbean Island of Guadeloupe. He returned to India after his five-year *Girmitiy*a tenure, and married a woman named Gulab. After some time, he wanted to go back. This time his destiny didn't take him to Caribbean but to Natal. Caribbean and South Africa are thousands of miles apart! I often wonder how in the nineteenth century an illiterate person managed to work in these far away corners of the world.

After his *Girmitiya* period in Natal was over, he started working at laying down railway tracks there. From a sugarcane field to laying railway tracks, he finally settled with a grocery store at Charlestown. Later he opened branches in Newcastle and Ingegane. Gradually this *Girmitya* grew so prosperous that he started trading horses. Gurdeen was also a part-time wrestler. He and Gulaba had sixteen children.

During this time, a lawyer from London, Mohandas Karamchand Gandhi, was leading an organized fight against the tradition of *Girmitiya* labour. Gurdeen would often meet him, and Gandhi asked him to organize a *Satyagraha* strike in Newcastle. It was owing to these strikes organized by likes of him, that in 1913 the *Girmitiya* tradition was stopped.

I tried to look for one temple built by Gurdeen in Newcastle, but sadly couldn't track it yet. There is an old Krishna temple there but not sure if it was built by Gurdeen. History keeps forgetting such people.[6]

First Coolie or First Slave

As soon as there is a mention of South Africa, the first man who comes to mind is Mohandas Karamchand Gandhi, the 'first *Girmitiya*', as he is referred by Indian author Giriraj Kishore.[7-8] But I will discuss

Gandhi less and discuss more about the people for whom Gandhi adopted the *Girmitiya* status and set out on a journey to become a Mahatma.

When did the first coolies arrive and why?

I found that the first Indian to probably reach Africa was the family of Kalga Prabhu in 1771. This may be factually incorrect, but his story is a legend now. Kalga Prabhu, a Gaur Saraswat Brahmin, was a prosperous trader from Cochin. He had so much influence that nobody dared to take cudgels against him. Once he got into a legal wrangle with a Rabbi (jewish priest) and the king of Cochin ruled against him. To avenge it, he began conspiring with the Sultan of Mysore, Haidar Ali, against the king of Cochin. King came to know about this, and took help of Dutch traders who took Kalaga Prabhu along with his family to the Cape of Good Hope. Keraleshwar temple in Cherlayi, Cochin was constructed by this Kalaga Prabhu.[9]

People had been brought to South Africa much before Kalga Prabhu came. A child named Aari was abducted when he was playing on the beach in Surat and brought here to Africa. Several other children too were here brought in this manner.[10] Evidently, it must have been easy to kidnap children and sell them as slaves.[11]

When I tried looking for any information about these slaves, I found a picture in the Rijks Museum in Netherlands, in which there were pictures of traders known as *Magh* from Arakan (Myanmar) selling slaves from Bengal. Dutch East India Company dispatched these young slaves from the Chittagong (now Bangladesh) via Masulipatnam to Batavia (Jakarta).[12] From there they were brought to the Cape of Good Hope. The first slave to be brought here is mentioned as 1658.[13] Later from the ports of Nagapattinam and Pulicat, 3,695 slaves were sent to Batavia.[14] Many of these slaves were Bengali women, who were given Christian names. These women were often shared mistresses of Dutch men.[15] Some of them were also bequeathed a lot of wealth. There is a mention of a Bengali women Anselia, who had so much wealth that Groot Constantia, the oldest wine estate of South Africa, belonged to her daughter.[16]

Girmitiya Ships

In 1849 a man named E.R. Rothbon started farming on five acres of land by the river Natal. He brought four labourers from Mauritius who were probably the first *Girmitiyas* of Africa. In my attempt to look for their names I came across a mention of one Babu Naidu who probably worked in the diamond mine at Kimberley. All this seems like a giant riddle, but it is for sure that their descendants are still there in Africa.[17-18]

Bonded labour began to be brought here in 1860. The first Girmitiya ship to reach South Africa named *Turo* sailed from Madras with 342 people. It had 190 adult males, 80 adult women and 72 children. Out of these, 163 were Hindus and the rest were Muslims and Christians. Later, ships began to arrive here from Calcutta. These voyages were short, about three weeks, but very rough. On board the *Belvedere* from Calcutta, 29 people died on the way.

Why Africa that was sending labour to the world had such shortage of labour in their own country? Sending Indian labourers to Africa did not seem logical. One possibility can be that the Zulu tribal people weren't fit for farming work. But the real reason was something else. Those days the Secretary of Natal, Shepstone passed a law that native Africans should live in segregated areas and made self-reliant. In such a situation, obviously there was a dearth of workers and thus brought from India.[19]

Between 1861 and 1867, 6450 Indians were brought here.[20] Some people came here just by chance. In 1865 a Girmitiya ship *Fusilier* going to Demerara began to sink near Africa. The passengers were rescued and brought to Natal. The labourers decided to stay back.[21] They barely cared if it was Guyana or Africa! In the next fifty years, about 1,50,000 labourers came to work in sugarcane fields in South Africa, mainly in the Natal region. About 60% of them were from Tamil and Telugu regions. 80% of them were Hindus and 15% Muslims.

These workers were recruited as per the *Girmitiya* contract for five years (Appendix 6). Since, many were from South India, modus operandi was different. I am citing an example.

Govind Swami Suppan was a surveyor in Madras railways and was also preparing for his Matriculation exams. His ambition was to become a teacher. One day he met an agent who told him that he would get him the same job in Africa with a better salary. Govind fell for it. When he reached Natal, he was sent to work in sugarcane fields. He had never done this kind of hard work before. He began to remain sick. Finally, due to some incident on the plantation, he was paralysed and sent back to India. He probably could never become a teacher.[22]

Here also the conditions of the barracks were pitiable and they were a hub of diseases. Indians weren't allowed to step out of the 3.2 km radius of the estate, without a permit. And of course, the fines and punishments were there for breaking the rules. Next to Fiji, the maximum deaths by suicide in any *Girmitiya* island was in the African plantations. Life in the estates of Reynold Brothers was exceptionally torturous.[23]

Once a manager Alexander asked a labourer from Gonda (U.P) to cut grass late at night. When he refused, he was kicked in the scrotum. Meanwhile his friends Brijlal and Budhri came there and the three started beating the manager. Finally, when Alexander begged for his life, they let him go. But they got scared that Alexander might get his friends or the police later. They bludgeoned him to death.[24]

Women Coolies of Africa

Contrary to other *Girmitiya* islands, African estates didn't encourage women labourers and preferred only men. They believed that if these coolies started families here, they would settle down here. A couple of Mulwa and Nutni came to Natal in 1879 and were assigned the same estate. Initially they were asked to live with a coolie named Puniya, where Nutni would have to do all household chores. Nutni got neither work nor wages. Mulwa didn't like that they had to share accommodation with another man. When he complained to the manager, they were forcibly made to stay with two men, Sahebdin and Murugeshan. One day his wife Nutni asked him, "Please go to work. If you don't, then who will give us food?"

When he returned to his barrack in the afternoon, he found his wife in a compromising position with Sahebdin. Enraged Mulwa killed her right there with an axe. Later he confessed his crime and narrated the entire course of events to the judge. The judge reluctantly sentenced him to death but remarked that if the conditions of the barracks remain the same, these kinds of crimes were bound to happen regularly.

Due to dearth of women in the plantations many cases of unnatural sexual violence were also noticed. At least two such incidents are reported where *Girmitiya* men were found to be sexually abusing animals. A *Girmitiya* said in some other context-

"We were considered animals in this bonded labour, so with time we also became animals."[25]

Eventually, the British government made a rule that for every 100 male labourers at least 40 women were to be sent to Natal. Indian women began to contribute a lot to sugarcane farming. In tea estates, they proved to be better than men. But women got only half the wages as men.

In 1885 a labourer named Ramdin lamented before the Wragg Commission-

"You people made me dine with people of different castes and now I am polluted. People in India wouldn't even let me sit and have a meal with them now. No amount of compensation can bring my caste back."

Ramdin had come from Bahraich in UP, and he had made good money in South Africa. After the death of his elder brother in India he brought his widowed sister-in-law to work in the fields here and later married her. Whereas on one hand, Ramdin found himself an outcaste in India, on the other hand he married a widow.

A Brahmin man Chhaju from Muzaffarnagar who lied to the Arkati that he was a *Jat* (farmer caste) and managed to reach Natal. When his father came to know, he wrote a letter to Calcutta that Chhaju must be summoned back. Chhaju was married with a wife still in the village, but he refused to return. Chhaju's father wrote back that his son has died for him. Whereas Chajju liked the farmer's life, two other Brahmins, Rabi Lal and Pawan Sukh refused to work in the fields. They were thus sent back to India.

There was no place for casteism in Africa, one could only survive by being casteless.[26]

Coolies' own Natal

After ten years these coolies had the option of returning to India, but most decided to stay back in Natal. Many of them had leased some land and begun cultivating fruits and vegetables. This business spread so fast that in 1885 in Natal alone there were 200 Indian fruit and vegetable vendors selling the produce which they grew on their own fields.[27]

In 1861 an Indian, Babu Naidu, opened a spice shop at Field Street, Durban.[28] After 1869, many Indians began coming to Durban. In 1872 Abu Bakr Ahmed Zaveri, a prosperous trader from India came to Natal. Many Memon traders followed him from Gujrat. Later, in 1877, many came to work in the diamond mines. These Gujaratis were mistakenly called Arabs by the Whites because they were Muslims. They wore *kurti* and *azar* and a Turkish hat on the head just like Arabs.[29] Whether Hindu or Muslim, these prosperous traders were not called coolie but referred to as 'passengers' because they had come to Africa at their own expense and not on any contract. They established their own business and began to compete with the Whites. They also recruited many Indian workers in their companies, often travelled to India and politically connected too. These traders have an enormous contribution towards the progress of Gujaratis in India.

In 1894 there were 46,000 Indians in Natal, whereas the number of Whites were 45,000. When they began giving tough competition to Whites, a rumour was floated that Indian traders were unethical who sold their products at less profit. The Whites also tried to keep their African customers happy by giving them cheap liquor. In 1893 barrister Mohandas Karamchand Gandhi came to Natal to fight a case for one Memon trader named Abdullah. He was hired on a fee of 140 pounds. Seth Abdullah's case was for the recovery of 40,000 pounds. It was in South Africa that Gandhi realized the extent of discrimination against Indians by the Whites.

When *Girmitiya* were freed, Indians began to progress in many ways in Africa. Their business flourished. In the 1870s freshwater fish business of Durban was the monopoly of Indians. According to a statistic from 1903, 87% workers in sugar mills and cleaning of cotton,

91% workers of tea and coffee industry and 82% workers of match factories were Indians. In 1902, 500 janitors and 20 police constables were Indians.[30]

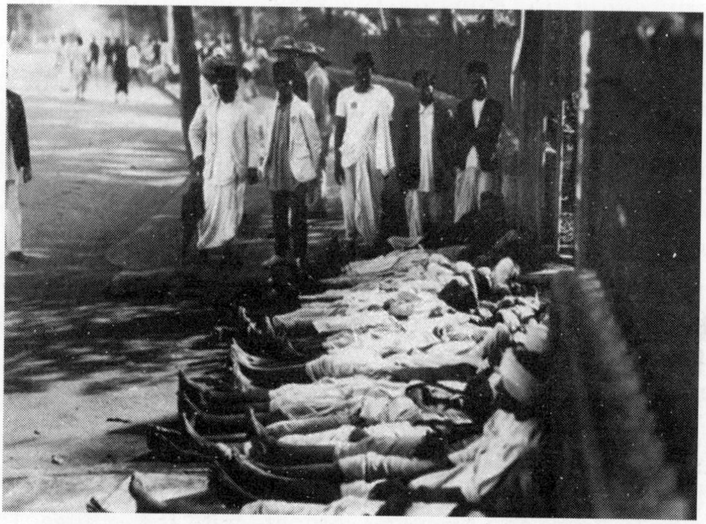

A strike in support of Gandhi in year 1930 (Courtesy- Wikimedia commons)

In 1869 the first wooden temple was constructed in Rosberg. Then one by one many temples came up in Natal. Today in the KwaZulu-Natal area, 72% are of Indian origin. Gauteng has 20% Indian blood. Similarly, Chatsworth, Phoenix and Lenasia have dense Indian population.

Uganda, Africa

"Some Asian people are rubbing shoe polish on their faces to look like us. There will be disciplinary action against them."

- Idi Amin

Kampala, 1972

Indians in western attire are standing in long queues. Many of them are Punjabi Sikhs, Gujaratis, Bengalis and Marathis. None of them look poor. This is a queue of affluent Indians who have come to buy flight tickets to leave this country. They bundled up all their stuff and moved to London, Amsterdam, Vancouver, and some to New Delhi. Many parcels were lying scattered on the airport floor.

Amidst this hullabuloo, somewhere in Kampala slums, children of black families are running around in rags. Some old people in their undergarments are smoking cigarette. Since all shops and factories are closed, they have nothing to do. Factory owners were leaving this country.

"These Indians have looted our country. These Patels and Shahs must leave. They have drained out all the wealth of out country and sent to India" an African young man shouts.

Meanwhile one prankster hurls a stone at an Indian shop. Soon many others join him in the hurling of stones. They pull down the billboard, and throw it away. A few Indians are standing close and watching helplessly. They know that their regime has ended. Africans who were their erstwhile servants would now take on their shops.

Ugandan dictator Idi Amin gave a 90-day ultimatum to all Asians. What would happen if they overstayed? Would they be executed or left to rot in jail? Or be thrown in the ocean?

When asked, Idi Amin had said laughingly, "Indians are good swimmers." [31-32]

Towards the end of the nineteenth century, the British contractor Ali Mullabhai Jivanji brought many Indians to Uganda, mostly Sikhs, to lay railway tracks. About 32,000 workers were brought and this work went on till 1935. Many of them died or returned to India but 6724 Indians stayed back.[33]

Whether in Canada or Africa, Sikhs were mostly chosen to lay railway tracks, because they were good with such mechanical skills. On the other hand, people from Bengal and Oudh were brought for farming. In the beginning of the twentieth century, many Gujaratis also came to Uganda. By 1970 Indian population there had increased to about 80,000. Most of them were affluent and a huge part of Uganda's economy. About 90% business was controlled by them. They used to literally rule over the blacks of Uganda and thus disliked by the natives.

In 1972 Idi Amin took over after a coup d'ètat and threw all Indians out of Uganda. Their money and property were sealed. Legally they could only take 50 dollars out of the country. 27, 200 people fleed to Britain, since they still were British citizens. 6,000 people went to Canada, 4,500 to India, 2,500 to Kenya and so on. Only a few Indians were left behind in Uganda with their homes, fields, shops, and businesses taken away. The 1976 film *Charas* was based on this event.

The economy of Uganda had collapsed after the Indians left. In 1986 when President Yoweri Museveni came to power, he invited the Indians to return to Uganda, promising to return their wealth and property. Idi Amin was exiled from the country, and he lived in Saudi Arabia till his death in 2003. Indians are again establishing themselves in Uganda. Sudhir Ruparelia was the first among those who had the courage to return to Uganda. Today he is one of the richest people in Uganda with wealth worth over 800 million dollars.[34]

Reference

1. Shekhar Bhatia, "Freddie Mercury's family tale of singer's pride in his Asian heritage", The Telegraph, 16October 2011
2. Richard F. Burton, *Zanzibar: City, Island and Coast, Vol.1*, Tinsley, London,1872
3. Richard F. Burton, First Footsteps in East Africa are an Exploration of Horror, Longman, Brown, Green and Longmans, 1856
4. Richard F. Burton, *First Footsteps in East Africa are an Exploration of Harror*, Longman, Brown, Green and Longmans, 1856

5. F.W.D Clark, *The Last Treack, A New Beginning,* St. Martin Press, 1999
6. J. Hoge, Personalia of the Germans at the Cape, 1652-1806, Cape Town, Ancestry 24,2004
7. Ashwin Desai and Ghulam Wahid, *Inside Indian Indenture: A South African Story*, 1860-1914, SHRC Press,2010
8. Giriraj Kishore, Pehla Girmitiya, Bhartiya Gyanpeeth,2011
9. Ramchandra Guha, *India Before Gandhi,* Penguin India, 2013
10. History of Gaur Saraswat Brahmins (Internet source)
11. Marius Francois Walkauf, New Light on Africans and Malays, Portuguese, Editions Peters, 1972
12. Enuga.S. Reddy, Indians in South Africa, A Little Known Aspect of Indian South African Relations, Articles, papers and speeches, November 1990
13. Will O Dik, An End of the *History of Silence: The Dutch Trade in Asian Slaves- Arkan and Bay of Bengal, 1621-1665,* International Centre for Asian Studies, Newsletter, 46
14. Parbawati Ram, A Forgotten Indian Diaspora: Forced Indian Migration to the Cape Colony 1658-1834, Doctoral Dissertation, University of Western Cape
15. Anshu Datta, From Bengal to The Cape: Bengali Slaves in South Africa from Seventeenth to Nineteenth Century, Jhilibris, 2013
16. Robert carl Hineshel, Slavery at the Cape of Good Hope, 1680-1731, Doctoral dissertation, Yale University
17. Gerald Granewald, Dynasty Building, Family Networks and Social Capital: Alcohol Pacters and the Development of the Colonial Elite at the Cape of Good Hope, 1760-1790, *New Country,* No. 62,2011
18. E.H.Brooks and Web, History of Natal, University of Natal Press,1979
19. Surendra Bhana and Joy Brian, Setting Down Roots: Indian Migrants in South Africa 1860-1911, Witwatersrand University Press, 1989.
20. Ibid.
21. David Northrop, *Indentured Labour in the Reign of Imperialism, 1834-1922*, Cambridge UniversityP, 1995
22. Surendra Bhana Ref. 15
23. Ashwin Desai Ref. 2
24. Surendra Bhana Ref. 15
25. Same Ref. 2
26. George Russell, The History of Old Durban and Reminiscences of an Immigrant of 1850, T W Gribbs, 1899
27. Surendra Bhana Ref. 15
28. Same Ref. 15
29. George Russell. The history of Old Durban and reminiscences of an immigrant of 1850. T. W. Griggs. 1899.
30. Surendra Bhana Ref. 15
31. ibid
32. Documentary telecast on Thames TV entitled "Uganda: Idi Amin Asian Expulsion, 1972".
33. Film *The Rise and Fall of Idi Amin* directed by Sharad Patel.
34. Melvin Amber and others, *The Encyclopaedia of Diasporas: Immigrant and Refugee Cultures Around the World, 2005.*
35. Farhana Dawood, "Ugandan Asians dominate economy after exile", BBC news, Kampala.

Canada

"Hindus are not suitable for the environment of this country."

– Mackenzie King, (Former Labour Minister, Canada)•

Sikhs of Sarabha

Sarabha is a Sikh village in West Ludhiana with about 700 households. Whenever I listen to the name of this village, I am reminded of Kartar Singh Sarabha from this village, who joined the Ghadar party in America when he was just 17. At the age of 19 he was hanged at Lahore Jail in 1915. Revolutionary icon Bhagat Singh considered him his Guru. This poem written by Kartar Singh had sowed the seeds of revolution back then-.

"Service of the country O my life is hard.
It is easy to mere talk
Those who have joined the service of the country
They have borne a million difficulties".[1]

Many years ago, there was a gathering in this village, where Sikh soldiers were surrounded by the villagers. They had just come back from a war abroad with many stories to tell. The country which they were telling a story about that day, was to become the future of millions of Punjabis in the coming decades.

These soldieres have returned from Canada, the snow-covered heaven where Queen Victoria ruled. A country that seemed like a dream. Miles of vacant land where multiple Punjabs could be settled.

• Quoted in 'The Karma of Brown Folk' by Vijay Prashad

Fields so huge that their boundaries were invisible from one spot. A land of peace and wealth. The villagers heard the stories and got back to their chores, but one teenager cherished the dream of Canada. He decided that he would surely go to Canada, and he started saving money for it.

In 1913 young Bagga Singh, leaving behind his wife and two daughters set out for Canada (British Columbia) on a ship. He promised them that he would one day return to take them along. The voyage to Canada was long and difficult but Bagga Singh wasn't alone. There were many other Sikh men with him. In those times, families weren't allowed in Canada.

After arriving in Canada Bagga Singh reached Westminster city. For many years, he kept working in one mill after the other, moving from one city to another. When Bagga Singh would return from the mill, sawdust would be stuck to his clothes and his body would stink of resin. Carrying a thick log of wood, he would return to his hut in the workers' colony to cook that day's meal. This continued for ten years. At last, he settled in a town called Paldi, which was settled by an affluent Sikh Mayo Singh. He, in fact, has named the town after his village Paldi from Punjab.

Bagga Singh was still a loner. He kept waiting for the day he could get his family here. After spending 17 years in Canada, he could finally get his family here. This isn't the story of just Bagga Singh but of all those Sikhs who came to Canada in those initial years, on whose foundation the Indian community in Canada stands today.[2]

Empress of Asia

Though in the 18th Century Portuguese and British armies had come from India to Canada, but I don't have any evidence that they started living in this cold place. It was Sikh battalion sent there in 1847, who started this trend.[3] At that time the Canadian government wanted people to settle there, fearing capture of their lands by Americans. Sikh Battalion returned to India, but they cherished Canada in their aspirations. As their pension was less, some of these army veterans came back to Canada and settled here. Gradually they began to call over relatives from Punjab. Since both India and Canada were under the British rule, this process was easy.

Railway tracks were being laid in Canada, and two big companies of Canada- Canada Pacific Railway and Hudson Bay Company badly needed labour. They began recruiting many Sikhs from India. Laying railway tracks in the biting cold wasn't an easy job. With snow all around and shivering cold, these Sikh men worked in extreme circumstances. They would cook *daal-chawal* on a wooden fire and sleep in their tents. At first, I was trying to segregate these stories from Girmitiyas but as I read further, I found these Canadian Sikhs much closer to *Girmitiya* coolies. Though they were never called one.

Canada was indeed different than Girmitiya countries because they had to manage this journey at their own expenses. Sikhs would bow their heads in their village's Gurudwara and board a train for Calcutta. In those days that journey would take about four days. Indians mostly travelled in 'third class' in those days. People from the Gurudwara waited at the Howrah station to take care of them. From Calcutta they would take a ship to Hong Kong. There were many cargo ships belonging to companies like *Dollar*, *Jardine*, and *Mckenzie*, which carried passengers in their basement. It took about 15-20 days to Hong Kong. There would be a stove on the ship where passengers would cook for themselves. Sikhs would pitch a tent to avoid rains and stormy waves. Their cooking vessels would often scatter helter-skelter, and they would have to chase around.

Ship would halt at Rangoon, Penang (Malaysia) and Singapore before finally reaching Hong Kong. Hong Kong had a Gurudwara where Sikhs could stay and eat the free *Langar* food. Here officials from Canada interviewed them and checked the documents. Many had to stay up to a year in Hong Kong for this process. Sometimes the papers of a husband would get approved, and the wife and children had to wait in Hong Kong longer. This must have been so difficult! But the solace was that the Gurudwara took the responsibility of taking care of them all. Finally, ship would leave Hong Kong for Vancouver, via Tokyo, Nagasaki, and Honolulu to Canada.

The most popular of the ships for Canada was- Empress of Asia.

In 1906-7, 4700 Indians reached Canada. How did the Whites there react to the arrival of these Sikhs? There were already African Blacks there, but these Sikhs were a different non-white race coming from a foreign land. In those days there were 'Whites only' cinema halls and hotels. Native White as well as Africans didn't like these newcomers and would often resort in beating them. At their arrival in 1907 there was a horrific riot where their homes and shops were attacked and damaged. In 1908 a despicable plan was made that all Indians (they were called Hindus) should be taken from Canada and discarded at Honduras. Fortunately, this didn't happen.

Gradually, Sikhs began to stabilise their presence. They first landed mostly in the British Columbia area. There in Vancouver in 1907 Vancouver Khalsa Deewan Society was established and the very next year the construction of the first Gurudwara was completed.

Indian immigration was curbed at in many ways. Between 1908 and 1919 Indians were prohibited from bringing women and children. In addition, there was a condition that any Indian coming here must get at least two hundred dollars with them. Many Sikhs began to return to India due to these stringent conditions and in 1914 there were only 2000 Indians remaining. Till 1957 one of the laws said that in a year only 100 Indians would be allowed.

Komagata Maru

The history of Canadian Indians is incomplete without the mention of this ship. This Komagata Maru ship that left Hong Kong in 1914 there were 376 Punjabi people.

This was a rebel ship in many ways. They were against the law that restricted the number of people allowed to be brough to Canada to one hundred annually. The person bringing this ship, Gurdit Singh Sandhu of Sarhali was a leader of the Ghadar party and was also supported by Barakatullah. It is quite possible that throughout the voyage there was sloganeering against the British and speeches invoking Sikh unity.

The passengers were stopped as soon as they reached Vancouver. Only twenty people could get down. Just twenty! Not even a hundred as per the law. Rest of them were falsely claimed to be suffering from an eye disease Trachoma and prohibited from getting down. The passengers were angered and decided to wage a legal battle from the ship itself. The ship remained halted for two months in Vancouver while the local Gurudwara managed their food supplies. Bagga Singh whom I have mentioned earlier formed a committee and supported the revolt from the coast.

It was relatively hot summer and the conditions on the ship were deplorable. At last Canadian government ordered that if the ship doesn't return, it must be blown up. Komagatu Maru had to return finally. When they returned to the Budge-Budge harbour in Calcutta they protested about the discriminatory behaviour of the British government. The mention of Budge-Budge also reminded me that this is where Swami Vivekanand landed after his return from Chicago. But that day it wasn't peaceful at all. When the British came to arrest Gurdit Singh, the agitated Sikhs attacked the officials. The British fired and 19

Sikhs on Komagatu Maru ship. Gurdith Singh Sandhu in white beard (Courtesy- Leonard Frank, Wikimedia commons)

people died. Some people say more than fifty Sikhs had died.[5] Gurdit Singh ran away. He surrendered later in 1922 after being inspired by Mahatma Gandhi.

Sikhs responded to The Komagata Maru incident differently. After a few days a Canadian officer William Hopkinson was murdered by Mewa Singh, who was punished later with death sentence. Probably this was the first hang till death punishment for a Sikh in Canada.

Birth of the Second Generation

In 1912 first Indian was born in Canada. He was Har Dayal Singh Atwal, the son of the first Granthi of the Gurudwara, Balwant Singh Atwal. Balwant Singh returned to India after a few years but what happened to him is indicative of the circumstances of those times. Since it was the time of *Ghadar*, Sikhs abroad were getting organized and revolting. Bombs were being made. Pilot trainings were being done. Young Sikhs were learning to fire a gun and were returning to Punjab as revolutionists. Every other Sikh abroad was being hunted down. The moment Balwant Singh Atwal returned on a ship, he was captured and imprisoned in Singapore jail. He kept saying that he is a *Granthi* (priest) but nobody listened to him. A letter was sent to Vancouver for enquiry but probably the letter never reached the correct address (or simply ignored). In 1917 Balwant Singh Atwal was hanged till death in Lahore Jail.[6] Who remembers these Sikh martyrs executed in Lahore jail? The first *Granthi* of Canada was hanged till death without any proven charges!

It became difficult for Sikhs to return to India during these uncertain times. While Chinese workers got permanent residence, Indians didn't get this status in Canada. When these Sikhs would return, get married or meet the family and then try to get back, they couldn't because of the lack of permanent residence certificate.

Sikhs stayed in Canada despite all difficulties. By 1920 many major cities like Westminster, Nanaimo, Golden, Abbotsford, Fraser Mill and Paldi had Gurudwaras. Sikh neighborhoods grew around these places.

Although many Sikhs quit Sikhism practices, chopped their hair, or became member of *sehajdhari sect.* Many married local Canadian people and permanently settled there.

I was curious, how could Sikhs settle there despite all the odds? This is the quality of the Sikh community that they struggle and strive always. In 1909 a former Harvard student Teja Singh came to Canada and decided to change the image of the Sikhs. He establishes a company from the Vancouver Gurudwara- Guru Nanak Mining and Trust Company. It had three aims: -

Creating an independent and strong identity of Sikhs, Hindus and Indian Muslims in America and Canada.

Bringing more and more families, wives and children and establishing more and more independent farming and businesses.

By becoming members of more and more companies and putting half the profits for religious and educational activities.

Teja Singh led the Sikhs and all Indians in Canada and submitted a memo to the officials.

One more advantage that worked in the favor of Sikhs was that they assimilated the Canadian way of life easily. Women started wearing Western dresses. Everybody learned English quickly. Many who had cut their long hair remained a Sikh in heart. They quickly brough them at par with Canadian citizens. This was possible due to an organized community, and this is what makes them different from other *Girmitiya* countries.

An inherent character Sikhs have even today that they don't consider any work lowly. Though they were a farming community, they were different than the feudal system in the rest of India. They were 'technically' supposed to be free of casteism, hence closer to the Western society in many ways. One of the first professions taken up by them was in wood mills. They would saw wood and sell it to companies. They bought machines, fields, trucks, and homes. Many of them were hard-working and skilled entrepreneurs. They constructed the Gurudwara in Vancouver by carrying big stones and putting them together themselves.

When Sikhs established their companies and factories, it opened more opportunity for Sikh labourers. The racial discrimination was lesser in Sikh owned firms. As a result, the Sikh community kept growing in numbers and prosperity. During the Great Depression in the 1930 Sikhs supported each other. Unemployed were given jobs and Gurudwaras provided food and shelter. If anyone needed money in Punjab (India), they sent them over from Canada. Gurudwara Management performed these duties with diligence.

By giving good English education to their children, they increased their employability. They were now not just labourers and farmers but contributors in Canada's overall progress. Although in the initial days, Whites wouldn't employ them on higher posts and even degree-holders carried wood in sawmills. But with time this attitude changed.

During the Second World war the Sikhs unknowingly chanced upon a treasure. Canadians chased away the Japanese who were part of the Axis powers. Although Sikhs didn't like exodus of their Asian brethren, but this increased their prosperity. Japanese sold their homes and property at lower rates, which were bought by the Sikhs.[7]

In 1947, four months before Indian independence the Canadian Indians too achieved a kind of freedom. They got the right to vote, which was double the joy for them. Canadian Sikhs were always connected with the happenings in Punjab. This was one reason why Canada supported the Khalistan movement, which took form of terrorism later.

Other than Sikhs, many Anglo-Indians and Christians from Goa came to Canada. They were scared that they would be expelled from India and Pakistan after the British exit. In the 70s people came from the exodus in Uganda by Idi Amin. *Girmitiya* descendents from Caribbean islands also came here. Canada abolished the limit on visa, and since the 90s about 30 to 40 thousand Indians began to come to Canada. Indians who were once a minority are on a path to become a majority, with about 1.4 million people of Indian origin in Canada (as per 2016).[8]

Reference

1. Bimanbihari Majumdar, India: Militant Nationalism in India 1897-1917, General Printers and Publishers, Calcutta, 1966
2. Lindley Tracy, A Scattering of Seeds: Creation of Canada, McArthur & company, 1999
3. Sarit Singh Jagpal, Becoming Canadians, Pioneer Sikhs in their own words, Harbour Publishing, 1994
4. Same ref. 3
5. Same ref. 3
6. Same ref. 3
7. Same ref. 3
8. Kavita Sharma, The Ongoing Journey: Indian Migration to Canada, Creative Books, 1997

Myanmar

"The one who goes to Java, never returns
If they do, they've enough for seven generations."
- Old Gujarati song written for Java (Indonesia)

Arakan is a beautiful southern province in Myamar bordering Mizoram (India) and Chittagong (Bangladesh). A river Naf runs between Chittagong and Arakan. Lying close to the Bay of Bengal, the region looks segregated from rest of Myanmar. The estate in Arakan and Rakhine was destined to be the workplace for many contact labourers from India.[1] Traders from India often travelled to Burma those days while the contract labourers came over for jobs, and many settled here. One of the popular rice exporter ports Sittwe had about 97% Indian population.

Kangni and Maistri

As per an available census (2013) about 4% population of Myanmar is of Indian origin, roughly same as in the 1872 census when 5% of population was Indian.

In 1885, after the third Anglo-Burman war the British had captured parts of upper Burma and later Southern Burma too. King Mindon Min and his son Thibaw had to give the administration in the hands of the British.[2] Around the same time British India was importing rice from America. Soon they began mass cultivation of rice in Burma with help of Indian labourers.

Surprisingly, these labourers came mainly from South India. The labourers who came there brought more people from their villages, and thus became recruitment agents. These agents were known as *Kangni* and *Maistri.*[3] Kangni were mostly from Tamil speaking community and dealt mostly Malay labour force. Maistri were from Telugu community, with focus on Myanmar.

Kangni would wear a turban, silk *kurta* and bedecked with ornaments. With such an opulence, they attracted the villagers. Entire families would go to Malay at their call. The journey was short, and families remained together so this was overall a pleasant experience. But some Kangni were corrupt and shrewd people. They bribed the officials, even abducted, and forcibly took labourers.[4]

Maistri had three categories. The lowest were Gang Maistri who headed a gang of 10-20 people. Several of these Gang Maistris were under a Charge Maistri, who were under Head Maistri.[5] These Maistri would first bring the labourers without any contract to Myanmar and then sell them to the owners for cheap. British preferred them over the expensive native farmers. The work in Burma was tough and needed strong-built workers. Hence mostly men were brought there. Male-female ratio dwindled from 80:1 to 250:1 at one time. Their life became difficult women. Some sex workers from Devadasi caste (*Kalvantalu/ Bhogam)* were brought to Rangoon to entertain the labourers.[6-7]

Initial contracts were for three years and seasonal. They would come only in the harvesting season and then return to India. In India they earned about seven-eight rupees per month whereas in Myanmar they earned about twenty-five rupees.[8] Many rice farms were owned by rich Tamil traders or *Nagarthars*, and thus they worked under Tamil masters only. Later Tamil Chettiyar moneylenders also came, who would lend money to these labourers albeit at high interest.

The production grew so much that the British started exporting rice. This led to the establishment of many ports at Yangon, Bassein, Sittwe and Mawlamyine. Almost all the labourers were Indian and the higher officials were British.

In Rangoon, the conditions of the labourers were deplorable. Some forty labourers were housed in a tin barrack surrounded by dirty drains. In rural areas conditions were better.

Till 1883 about 85,000 Indians came to Burma.[9] This migration continued till 1938 and about 2.5 million Indians worked in Burma.

From Burma to Myanmar

The anti-Indian sentiments began to grow among natives after 1930. Burmese were fighting for independence against the British. Revolts against the British regime did affect the Indians labourers. The worst time for Indians was between 1942 and 1945 when Japan captured Burma.

Many Chettiar money lenders left Burma in fear. About 100,000 Indians ran away, while many died during the journey. Those who remained in Rangoon, joined Indian National Army, and joined hands with the Japanese army. This worked in their disfavour as the Burmese hated the Japanese army. Indians had to pay the price for Burmese nationalism. As soon as Burma was independent there were stronger laws for those coming from India.

The land of Chettiyar money lenders was taken away and they were given a small amount of compensation. Although a rule was made that those who have lived in Burma for more than eight years could be granted Burmese citizenship. But the Indians were insecure, and many didn't even apply for the citizenship. Even among the 400,000 Indians who applied, only 10,000 were granted citizenship.

The government also ruled that government jobs shall be given out only to Burmese people. All Indian employees from railways, ships and post-offices were also sacked. They were also prohibited from taking the money back to India. They even snatched necklaces of women who were travelling to India. They returned home empty-handed and till date are pleading with the Burmese government. As per a statistic since 1963, 1,44,352 Tamils have returned to India.

In Myanmar, people of Indian origin are not called a racial minority but a foreign minority. They don't have resident rights. Indians of Myanmar criticized Prime Minister Nehru as he did nothing to get them their rights, even when Burma became a part of the Non-Aligned Movement. On the other hand, people of Chinese descent had all the rights. Even the Prime Minister elected in 1962 Ne Win was of Chinese origin.

Indians had become a strange kind of slaves. According to the report of the Singhvi Committee about 400,000 Indians in Burma are stateless, having no citizenship anywhere. They neither have the permission to go to India nor do they have any citizen rights in Myanmar. They have no identity.

Once among the richest, Indians turned into the poorest community in Myanmar. Indians were either Hindus or Muslims while people in Myanmar were Buddhists. Due to this, personal relationships and marriages were negligible.

The Tamil people had opened many Tamil schools, which were closed later. Only Burmese medium schools remained. But the Tamils never protested and rather chose to live like natives. Tamil children would go to Burmese schools, eat food like them and play with them. On several occasions they even wore the traditional dress. Gradually they lost touch with the traditions of their own ancestors.

Myanmar has about a thousand Hindu temples with many native devotees. Many Hindu temples carry a Buddha statue, such that nobody would dare to demolish it. This was a smart move by the Tamils. After Tamil schools were closed, they continued teaching Tamil language, culture, dance, music in temples. Yet Tamils remained largely detached in this closed country. Many of the new generation has never seen India.

Biharis of Zayawaddy

Wide concrete paths amidst greenery, rickshaw driver wearing a conical hat, Burma's wooden huts and amidst these some concrete homes. Men with shirts tucked in their *lungis* and saree-clad women taking children to school. Zayawaddy, a cluster of villages between Yangon and Mandalay, where lives a small India.

Here about 70,000 people live have come from Bihar and Uttar Pradesh. The responsibility to get labourers from Bihar was on the Raja of Dumraon Keshav Prasad Singh, whom the Britishers gave 20 thousand acres of land on lease for thirty years. He handed over the responsibility to his *dewan* Harihar Prasad Singh. The first consignment of 3500 labourers came in 1889. In 1902 the second consignment brought about 4000 people. These labourers also underwent an interview where anyone who could count to ninety or hundred was selected. At that time this area was a dense forest with wild animals. These people had to cut those trees to start farming. Later Myanmar's first sugar factory was also started here.

The number of Bihari famers and labourers kept growing and they settled about forty villages which were divided into four hamlets- Jaipur, Ramnagar, Sadhugaon and Gopalganj. Teachers were also called from Bihar, but education was only up to primary level. There is a mention of inspector Pandit Lalu Ram Pandey who was brought here to maintain discipline. During the world war Subhash Chandra Bose came to Zayawaddy and some people joined his Indian National Army. Later, Indian Prime Minister Lal Bahadur Shastri also visited Zayawaddy once.

They were not as well off as the Tamils. Being poor and devoid of power, they easily got the citizenship of Myanmar. They have a Hindu Kalyan Sehyog Samiti there and Hindi is taught at the Gandhi Hall. There are about a hundred schools and a branch of the Rastriya Swayamsevak Sangh- Sanatan Dharma Swayamsevak Sangh. Indian television soaps are watched a lot. Sweets were distributed when Narendra Modi ji was elected the Prime Minister. But they don't want to return to India now. After the Imphal-Mandalay bus service, one may expect a reconnect in future.[10-11]

Malaysia and Singapore

9th July 1850

A chartered ship Mohammed Shah sailed from Calcutta to Singapore and two Sikhs alighted- Maharaj Singh and Khadak Singh. They might have been first immigrant Sikhs in Singapore. Maharaj Singh didn't come as a *Girmitiya* but as a prisoner accused of revolt against the British government. Sikhs call him one of the first Indian revolutionary. Although Maharaja Ranjit Singh and Bir Singh had fought earlier with British, but Maharaj Singh was a revolutionary in true sense. He invocated Sikhs with fiery speeches and created his own army. He was sent to a jail in Singapore, where he took his last breath.

A friend of mine in Singapore General Hospital narrates a beautiful incident. Once upon a time, there was a stone grave at the hospital. After the Second World War, some Tamils noticed it and began to offer flowers. Some Muslims thought this was a tomb and they followed the suit. Later Sikhs constructed a Gurudwara there and call it a grave of Maharaj Singh![12]

Girmitiya of White Gold

Malaysia and Singapore are one of the common destinations for Indians, ranging from IT professionals to mafia dons like Chhota Rajan. The arrivals of Indians in Malay (present day Malaysia) began centuries ago at the time of Emperor Ashoka and Chandragupta, but I shall focus only on the period of Colonialism. Whether contractual labourers or *Girmitiyas* came here?

South Indians had some experience of rubber plantations, so they were preferred.

British Army captured Penang peninsula and by 1909 they ruled over entire Malay.[13] This area was considered fit for growing sugar, coffee, spices, and white gold i.e., rubber. Thousands of hectares of land were vacated for agriculture. Forests were cut, homes were displaced. That is when these labourers were needed. According to Sandhu between 1896 and 1910 about 4.2 million Indian labourers came here at different times.[14] Many chose to return while many died. About 1.2 million Indians stayed back in Malay, with the number dwindling to about 0.8 million in 1957. Out of them, 0.5 million were born in Malaysia.[15]

The British brought Indians to do menial jobs. They didn't want them to progress.[16] Laws were made such that the workers could not even ask for better wages. Although the British made a lot of money from the rubber plantations. In 1947 they had net earning of about 151 million pounds. Malay was termed the biggest rubber factory in world.

But the labourers didn't get any share of this earning and remained in miserable condition.[17]

British managers were shrewd administrators. They took the responsibility of the safety and pensions for Malay kings, just like they did with Indian kings. In return, kings kept their people in control. Malay's native farmers were encouraged to grow rice, which provided food for the Indian and Chinese labourers. Since Indian labourers cultivated cash crops and Malay farmers cultivated rice, there was no conflict.

Rubber plantations had European managers at the top followed by Malyali and Sinhali supervisors, and the lowest rung were Tamil labourers. White Managers lived separately, but supervisors and labourers were in close and regular contact. The Malyali/Sinhali supervisors were educated and had good wages. They sent their children to English schools, and they made good progress as compared to the Tamil labourers. Tamil children were provided Tamil medium schools but only up to sixth standard. They were groomed to work on the rubber plantations.[18] The British government ensured that Tamil and Chinese labourers don't mingle with each other and kept them as separate as they could. Indians received a fixed salary, while Chinese labourers received incentive-based salary. Due to this there was a huge gap in the income of the two groups. Although All-Malayan Rubber Worker Council had members from both the groups.

Foreign Land of the Tamils

Indian Tamils never got Malay citizenship. As a result, their next generation couldn't become citizen either and continued to live there illegally. They didn't receive basic government facilities like education. Lack of education pushed many of them into the world of crime, with jails full of Indians. They got involved in theft, swindling, robbery, and drug rackets. Roots of this evil remain in the discriminatory behavior of the British who never granted Indians their rights.

During the second world war the condition of Malaysian Indians was terrible. Factories were closed and Tamils were begging on the roads.

When the British army was defeated by the Japanese army, the tables turned. Indians and Malay natives began believing that the British could be defeated. Some Indians got recruited in Indian National Army under Subhash Chandra Bose. Though they were disillusioned soon after. The Japanese were even more cruel than the British. They put them to construct the Siam-Burma railway track, in which many died. At last, they understood their mistake and started fighting against the Japanese.

Malay Communist Party organized the Chinese and Indian labourers for revolt. Malay Natives, people of Chinese origin and Indians joined hands to raise an army- Malay Anti-Japanese Army. These 20,000 people created 7 regiments and fought 282 wars at different places in which they killed about 5000 Japanese soldiers. When Japan surrendered on 15th August 1945 it was due to their global defeat, but the people of Malay got confident that they can defeat any major power in the world.

When the war was over the British returned to Malay with fanfare. Malay was a huge source of income for them, and they didn't want to let it go. Revolting labourers were labelled as terrorists by the government and they crushed them. They used their old tactic of divide and rule between the natives and the Immigrants. They made a law that would give the Indians and the Chinese equal rights and citizenship as locals.

Malay natives opposed it, and the labour unions split. There was a new wave of nationalism pitching natives against the immigrants. The British wanted this split to happen, and then they retracted the law. The rights of natives were increased and that of outsiders were curbed. This split between the natives and the immigrants shall be seen for decades to come.

When there was countrywide strike against the British, they imposed Emergency in 1948. This continued for 12 years becoming the longest emergency in the era of colonialism! All protestors were arrested, labour unions were banned, and many strict laws were made. This Emergency continued till 1960. Malaysia became independent in 1963 but Indians could never get their rights.[19]

About four decades later 20th November 2007, about 20,000 Tamil Indians of Malaysia marched to the British Embassy to give a memorandum to the Queen of England. In this HINDRAF March they asked for accountability for their oppression in 150 years.

Malaysia is a country with skyscrapers now. Slums and huts are being broken. Indian establishments and even their small temples are being demolished. A Tamil kid was running on this rubble from one mound to another. He was looking for some of his treasure buried in this rubble. An old temple constructed by some Tamil farmer was shattered, and the kid was looking for the statue of his goddess. As he found her head, he began jumping with joy![20]

Reference

1. Medha Chaturvedi, Indian Migrants in Myanmar: Emerging trends and challenges, Ministry of Indian Overseas Affairs
2. Douglas M. Peers, Anglo-Burmese Wars, Blackwell Publishing, 2011
3. Medha, Ref.1
4. Adapa Satyanarayana, Birds of Passage: Migration of South Asian labour communities to South Asia, Nineteenth-Twentieth Century, A.D. Clara working paper 11, Amsterdam, 2001.
5. C. Kondapi, Indians Overseas 1838-1949, Indian Council of World Affairs, New Delhi, 1951
6. Michael Adas, Economic Development and Social Change on an Asian Rice Frontier, 1852-1941, University of Wisconsin Press, 1974.
7. Medha, Ref.1
8. Adapa, Ref.4
9. Kondapi, Ref. 5
10. K. Keshavpani and others, Rising India and Indian communities in East Asia, Institute of Southeast Asian studies,2008.
11. Sonu Trivedi, The Indian Story in Myanmar, The Tribune, 12 September 2017.
12. Choor Singh, Bhai Maharaj Singh, The Saint Soldier, Singapore
13. Karnal Singh Sandhu, Coming of Indians to Malaysia, 1993
14. Same Ref. 2
15. Patricia Annamaria Spencer, Malayas Indian Tamil Labour Diaspora: Colonial Subversion of their quest for agency and modernity, Graduation thesis, Secondary source
16. Sandhu Ref. 2
17. D. J. M. Tate, The Malaysian Indians: History, Problems, and Future, Information and Research Development Centre, Malaysia, 2008
18. Spencer Ref.4
19. Same Ref. 4
20. Journeyman Pictures documentary, 'Are Malaysians being treated as second class citizens'

Appendices

1. Immigration Embarcation Certificate

Ship DINAPORE

Name	Oree
Father's name	Bhowanidin
Age	21
Caste	Bania
Height	5ft, 7½ ins
Name of next of kin	Bro' Rambocus
If married to whom	-------------------
Zilla	Barabunky
Pergunnah	Sunnoighat
Village	Tekaitnugur
Bodily Marks	Scar outside of shin

We certify that the man above described (whom I have engaged as labourer as the part of British Guiana where he has expressed his willingness to proceed to work for Hire), has appeared before me and that I have explained to him all the matters concerning his duties as an emigrant, according to Section 38, of all India Emigration Act vii of 1871.

Countersigned

---------------------------	----------------------------
Protectors of Emigrants at Calcutta	Emigration agent for British Guiana

Source: Basdeo Mangru, *Benevolent Neutrality, Indian Government policy and Labour Migration in British Guiana 1854-1884* (London, Hansib, 1987) 242

2. Kunti's Letter

The writer is Kunti, daughter of Charan Chamar of Lakhuapur P.O. Belghat, district Gorakhpur.

She left her home with her husband named Jal and went to Gorakhpur where a coolie emigration agent induced them by holding out tempting offers to have them registered for emigration to the Fiji Island and took them to Calcutta where he left them in the emigration depot. They had to live there amidst great difficulties for some days after which they were huddled with other immigrants into a steamer bound for Fiji. When the steamer reached Suva in the island they were taken out and were huddled like sheep into a boat and were taken to depot named Nukulau. Whence she and her husband were sent to a firm named Wini Wakasi in district Rewa. She worked there with her husband for four years and was able to maintain her chastity although with great difficulty. Now the sardar and the overseer desired to violate her chastity.

There is great difficulty in procuring evidence for all were afraid of the sardar. When the sardar and the overseer desired to violate the chastity of any woman they allotted work to her in a lonely place, where no evidence could be procured. A similar procedure was adopted when they wanted to beat any coolie. Under such circumstances several persons committed suicide or drowned themselves into a river.

On 10 April 1913, she was sent to work in an out-of-the-way field alone. The sardar and the overseer came there bent on violating her chastity. When the sardar attempted to get hold of her hand she ran away in utter despair and plunged into the river but was rescued by a boy in his boat and landed on the other shore. When she referred the matter to the owner of the firm, he refused to listen to her.

Now both she and her husband were being treated with greater harshness by the sardar and the overseer and were allotted extremely hard tasks. She and her husband were required to work separately at a distance of one mile from each other. She said that she was prepared to commit suicide if she found it impossible to maintain her chastity.

The woman concluded the letter with a warning to such Indian women as might, like her, be tempted to go to Fiji and with stirring appeal to the leaders of this country to try to put a stop to emigration to the Fiji Islands.

(This Letter was first published in 1913 in 'Bharat Mitra' titled 'The Cry of An Indian Woman in Fiji)

(Tears in Paradise: Sufferings and Struggles of Indians in Fiji, 1979-2004- Rajendra Prasad)

3.

Colony	Years of agreement	Total displaced *Girmitiya*
Mauritius	1834-1900	453,063
British Guyana	1838-1916	238,909
Trinidad	1845-1916	143,939
Jamaica	1845-1915	36,412
Grenada	1856-1885	3200
St. Lucia	1858-1895	4350
Natal	1860-1911	152,184
St. Kitts	1860-1861	337
St. Vincent	1860-1880	2,472
Reunion	1861-1883	26,507
Suriname	1873-1916	34,304
Fizi	1879-1916	60,965
East Africa	1895-	32,000
Seychells	?-1915	6315
Total		1,119,4357

- Reunion -75000 (14)
- French Caribbean- 7900 (14)
- Natal- 153000 (14)

- Burma- 1164000 (14)
- Ceylon (Sri Lanka)- 2321000 (14)
- Malay- 175400 (14)

(**Source :** Brij. V. Lal. Girmitiyas. The Origin of Fiji Indians. Journal of Pacific History, 1983)

4. Girmitiya Districts

1. United Province- Faizabad, Gonda, Baliya, Gazipur, Azamgarh, Basti, Gorakhpur, Benares, Mirzapur, Lucknow, Kanpur, Allahabad, Agra, Jaunpur, Kanpur.
2. Bihar- Shahabad, Patna, Gaya, Saran, Muzaffarpur, Champaran.
3. Punjab- Ambala, Rohtak and Delhi.
4. Central Province- Raipur, Bilaspur, Jabalpur.
5. Madras Province (Tamil)- Madras, Tanjore, Trichinopoly, South Arcot, Chingelput
6. Madras Province- Ganjam, Rajmundri, Vishakhapatnam, Godavari

5. Native Indian places of *Girmitiyas* in Fiji

1. Basti- 6815
2. Gonda-3589
3. Faizabad- 2329
4. Sultanpur-1747
5. Azamgarh-1218
6. Gorakhpur-1683
7. Allahabad-1218
8. Jaunpur-1188
9. Shahabad-1128
10. Rai Bareli-1087
11. Gaya-765

12. Patna-654

(Brij.V.Lal. Girmitiyas. The Origin of Fiji Indians. Journal of Pacific History, 1983)

6. Notice : Immigration Department

NOTICE TO COOLIES INTENDING TO EMIGRATE TO NATAL

You will be taken free of expenses to Calcutta, and, while there will be well fed and properly lodged till the ship sails; and should you be ill, the greatest care will be taken of you.

When the ship is ready, you will be supplied with good clothing; the finest ships are selected, and the voyage takes about five or six weeks. The food, medicines, and other appliances onboard are of good quality, and your health, comfort, and safety, will be most carefully attended to. The Indian government has appointed officers, who are most strict and vigilant in securing for you all these advantages.

On and after your arrival in Natal, there is a protector of Immigrants ready to advise at all times during your residence there. You will be located on an estate where a medical man is employed.

Your religion will in no way be interfered with, and both Hindoos and Mahomedans are alike protected.

You will find over 5,000 of your countrymen settled there.

You will have a house rent free to live in, with plenty of garden ground to cultivate at your leisure, and care is taken not to separate families and relatives.

The climate is remarkably healthy, and there is abundance of good water, fruits, and vegetables. If you are ill, medical attendance, medicines, and nourishment are provided free of charge.

You will be required to cultivate sugar-cane, and to make sugar, rum, and molasses. Great varieties of work, either for strong men or for women and children, are available.

You will have to work for five years, six days in the week, for nine hours, between sunrise and sunset- all Sundays and holidays excepted.

Besides rations the men receive for the first year, Rs.5 monthly; for the second year, Rs. 5 ½ monthly; for the third year, Rs. 6 monthly; for the fourth year, Rs.6 ½ monthly; for the fifth year, Rs. seven monthly. The women are paid half wages and the children in proportion.

After five years you may return to India at your own expense, and after ten years you will be entitled to a passage back.

You will receive rations as follows: -

1 ½ lbs. of rice daily, or for three days in a week in lieu of rice 2 lbs. of

Dholl .... 2 lbs. per month.

Salt fish............ 2 " " "

Ghee or oil......... 1 " " "

Salt.................. 1 " " "

H.A. Firth, Emigration Agent of NATAL

8, Garden Reach, Calcutta, 21st March, 1874.

(Source: Ashwin Desai and Goolam Vahed. *Inside Indian Indenture. A South African story. 1860-1914.* HSRC Press. 2010.)

7. Mahatma Gandhi's message to the Indians in Suriname

Pandit Bhawanibeekh Misra from Dutch Guiana met me with Shri Benarsidas Chaturvedi and asked for a message from me for the migrated brothers of Suriname. I only request you all that you must stay united, use Hindi- Hindustani language in your conversations with each other, open Hindi libraries and school.

M. K. Gandhi

Maganvadi, Vardha

11 October, 1935

(Excerpt from Pandit Shri Mishra's biography, *Dreamz World*, June 2018)

8. Girmitiya Songs

Bidesiya

a)

The Ship had come from the east and the west, it took away my husband the train has become my soutan, it took away my husband

b)

We left India O babua for the hunger
we were cheated and left the city of Patna
we lost the lap of mother Ganges
I didn't listen to my father-brother at all
O babua for the hunger!

(M. Mojumder, Kahe Gaile Bidesh: Why did you go Overseas? On Bhojpuri migration since the 1870s and contemporary culture in Uttar Pradesh and Bihar, Suriname and Netherlands. Suriname Resource Book of the Bidesia Project. 2010)

Birha

c) Riddle-

Which cow has twelve breasts and three hundred and sixty teats
Anyone who can understand my birha should sing along with me

One year has twelve months and days are three hundred and sixty
I do understand your birha o friend, you sing along with me.

d) Meeting of Rama and Krishna

Rāma, in your garden (is) Sītā's flower-bed -
(Where) (her) devar, Laksmasa, sits keeping guard.
He picks and picks tender lemons & sends them to susrāl;
Of these very lemons, a curry is made.
Krsna, the enemy of Murā, has sat to dine -
And Sītā fans (with a) whisk.

Marsiya (An elegiac poem)

e) *Where did your birth taken place, Hasan, (and) where was your umbilical cord cut?*

Where did you play ball, Hasan, (and) where did you lose your life?

My birth took place at Makkā (Mecca) (or) Madīnā (Medina) (and my) umbilical cord was cut on earth.

I played ball in the courtyard, mother, (and) lost (my) life in (the battlefield of) Qarblā.

(Usharbudh Arya. Ritual Songs and folk songs of the Hindus of Suriname.1968)

Pt. Chandra Shekhur Sharma

पं० चन्द्र शेखर शर्म्मा

ब्राह्मन ठाकुरबाड़ी, बक्शीगिरि, मेटियाबुज.

पो० गार्डेन रीच, कलकत्ता।

BRAHMAN THAKURBARI, MATIABRUZ, P.O. GARDEN REACH,

CALCUTTA, ता. १६ / १२ / 193६ ई.

प्रिय पुत्र परमानन्द सपरिवार को हमारे तरफसे प्रेम पूर्वक
शुभाशीरवाद स्वीकारहो,
आगे समाचार यह है कि हमारा जहाज सकुशल ता. १९ गुरुवार को नवम्बर
कलकत्ता पहुंचा, बादको शुक्रवारसे सोमवार ता. 23 तक यात्री उतरते रहे,
हममें तारीख 22 रविवार को जहाजसे उतर कर [illegible] और आपसमा
[illegible] पहुंच गया, बादको उपर [illegible] पर [illegible]
[illegible] कर रहे है, आजकल सरदी का मोसम है, पर कलकत्तामे सरदी बहुत -
कम होती है, ओढने के लिये एक ऊनी कम्बल और एक चद्दर से काम चल
जाता है। पर भीतर भारत वर्षमे ज्यों ज्यों [illegible] तरफ बढते जावो -
त्यों त्यों शीत अधिक पड़ती है ओढना बिछौना बहुत सा कपड़ा होना पड़ता है
इसी से [illegible] अभी मैं कलकत्ता से बाहर नहीं गया, और न जानेकी इच्छा है।
अब रही जहाजको [illegible] बाबू [illegible] के जामाता मि. परसाद और
हमारे [illegible] के मित्र डिस्पेन्सर मि. [illegible], और [illegible] डिस्पेन्सर बाबू
[illegible] चरन, और बाबू महाबीर सिं वगैरह को [illegible] प्रकार को खाने पीने

A letter from girmitiya Chandrashekar Sharma (Courtesy- Chan Choenni)

Chandrashekhar sharma, a Girmitiya from Suriname who returned rich and stayed in India (Courtesy- Chan Choenni)

Girmitiya women from Trinidad (Courtesy- Carribean hindustani

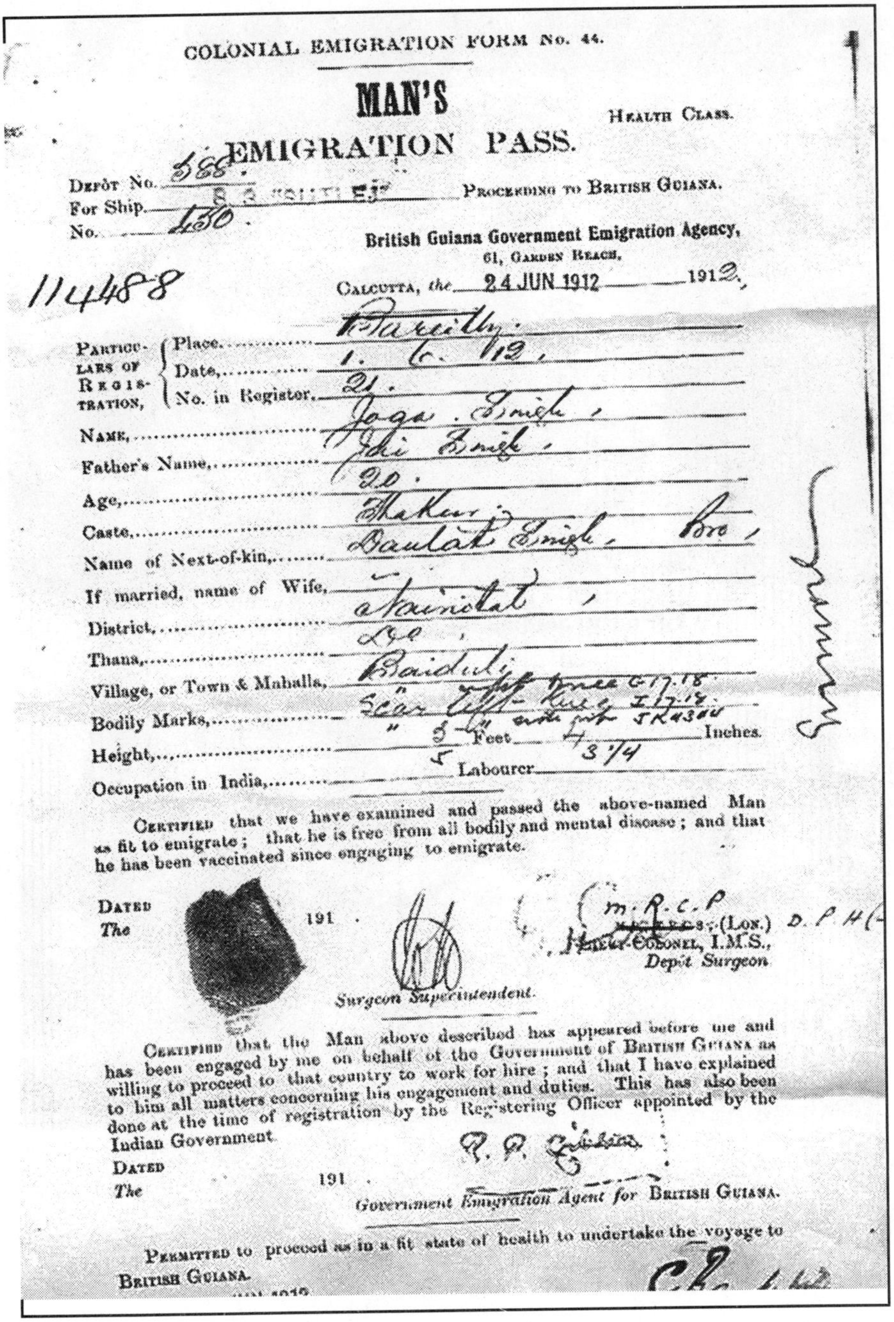

COLONIAL EMIGRATION FORM No. 44.

MAN'S

HEALTH CLASS.

EMIGRATION PASS.

Depôt No. 588.
For Ship. S. S. [illegible] Proceeding to British Guiana.
No. 450.

British Guiana Government Emigration Agency,
61, Garden Reach,

114488

Calcutta, the 24 JUN 1912 1912.

Particulars of Registration, { Place. Bareilly.
Date, 1. 6. 12.
No. in Register, 21.

Name, Joga. Singh.
Father's Name, Jai Singh.
Age, 20.
Caste, Thakur.
Name of Next-of-kin, Daulat Singh. Bro.
If married, name of Wife, —
District, Nainital.
Thana, Do.
Village, or Town & Mahalla, Baidul.
Bodily Marks, Scar left knee.
Height, 5 Feet 4 3/4 Inches.
Occupation in India, Labourer.

Certified that we have examined and passed the above-named Man as fit to emigrate; that he is free from all bodily and mental disease; and that he has been vaccinated since engaging to emigrate.

Dated
The 191

Surgeon Superintendent.

M.R.C.P. (Lon.) D.P.H.
Colonel, I.M.S.,
Depôt Surgeon

Certified that the Man above described has appeared before me and has been engaged by me on behalf of the Government of British Guiana as willing to proceed to that country to work for hire; and that I have explained to him all matters concerning his engagement and duties. This has also been done at the time of registration by the Registering Officer appointed by the Indian Government.

Dated
The 191

Government Emigration Agent for British Guiana.

Permitted to proceed as in a fit state of health to undertake the voyage to British Guiana.

A Girmitiya pass (Courtesy - Romola Lucas)

A Girmitiya outdoor kitchen (Courtesy- Archive)

Hanuman Temple, Chaguanas, Trinidad (May 2007)

□□